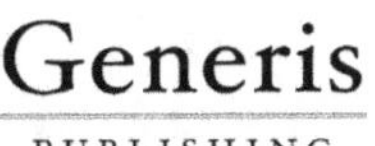

AF593332

Physical Facilities and Effective Educational Provision in Kenya

Mwangi Ndirangu

Copyright © 2025 Mwangi Ndirangu
Copyright © 2025 Generis Publishing

All rights reserved. This book or any portion thereof may not be reproduced or used in any manner whatsoever without the written permission of the publisher except for the use of brief quotations in a book review.

Title: Physical Facilities and Effective Educational Provision in Kenya

ISBN: 979-8-89248-790-0

Author: Mwangi Ndirangu

Cover image: https://pixabay.com/

Publisher: Generis Publishing
Online orders: www.generis-publishing.com
Contact email: info@generis-publishing.com

Table of Contents

Chapter 1

Educational Provision for Academically Gifted Children in Kenyan Public Secondary Schools

Gifted education has gained traction worldwide due to the recognition that gifted and talented individuals contribute significantly to human development through their innovations, leadership, and problem-solving capabilities (Shavinina, 2019). Failure to adequately support such learners, both globally and in Kenya, often leads to societal losses through academic underachievement, frustration, and disengagement. Gifted education is not just about academic excellence; it is also about harnessing diverse talents that can drive economic growth, innovation, and leadership. As Luvinzu (2021) argues, future problem solvers and innovators emerge from those identified and nurtured early in their educational journey. Young individuals who are academically talented and empowered as entrepreneurs will be the key drivers of Africa's and Kenya's global competitiveness (USAID, 2023).

There are no current statistics on the prevalence of gifted and talented learners in Kenya's school system. However, Kang'ethe and Karugu (1995) estimated them to be 3% of primary school learners at that time. In a study on educational provision for gifted learners in Nyandarua County, 6% of the primary school pupils were identified as gifted (Ndirangu, Mwangi & Changeiywo, 2007). A national study is needed to determine the exact proportion of gifted learners in the country.

Kenya has produced many bright minds, such as the late Calestous Juma. Juma was a prominent, internationally recognized scholar known for his ground breaking contributions to science, technology, and sustainable development, particularly in Africa. He was a professor at Harvard University's Kennedy School and a member of the U.S. National Academy of Sciences. His work on technology and agricultural innovation earned him numerous awards, such as the 2017 Breakthrough Paradigm Award. Known for his influential publications and advocacy for inclusive innovation, Juma played a vital role in advancing scientific and technological progress to address development challenges in Africa (Nordling, 2017).

Another gifted Kenyan, Nora Okong'o, an academically talented girl, joined the U.S. National Aeronautics and Space Administration (NASA) as a top scientist at the California Institute of Technology. She worked in the Jet Propulsion Laboratory (Ndirangu et al., 2007). A more recent case is that of a five-year-old boy, Elias Muthomi Gitonga, who has shown remarkable brilliance for his age. Reportedly, he could read at the age of two without formal education and had a high degree of understanding beyond that of his peers. At six, Gitonga was honored in the United Arab Emirates as one of the 100 exceptionally gifted children globally, in recognition for his knowledge of aviation (Lisumba, 2022).

Gifted Learners and Kenyan Public Schools

The Kenyan public school system currently has limited provisions for gifted learners, lacking structured policies, resources, and trained personnel to support their needs adequately. Teachers in regular schools often lack awareness of the specific needs and characteristics of gifted students. Many educators receive minimal training on how to identify or support these learners, which hinders the implementation of Individual Education Plans (IEPs) or enrichment programs. As a result, gifted learners are often managed within the standard curriculum without tailored interventions to maximize their potential (Matilda, Kariuki & Omulema, 2019). Reid and Horváthová (2020) note that specialized teacher training is essential for identifying and supporting gifted learners, yet Kenyan teacher education does not prioritize this. The National Association for Gifted Children (NAGC) in the United States emphasizes the importance of equipping teachers with the skills to create a challenging learning environment for gifted students. Kenyan teacher education programs should integrate these concepts to support gifted learners better (Wormald, 2017).

Kenya's Sessional Papers No. 14 of 2012 proposed the need to develop strategies to identify and nurture gifted learners. However, little action to actualise this has followed this far. Teachers rarely receive support from educational resource centres, and specialized tools for assessing giftedness are underutilized or unavailable, leading to inconsistent identification and support for gifted learners in mainstream schools (Matilda, Kariuki & Omulema, 2019).

Gifted Education and Vision 2030

Gifted education in Kenya can significantly support Vision 2030 by advancing human capital, fostering innovation, and promoting equity. By nurturing exceptional skills, gifted programs help create a skilled workforce, aligning with Vision 2030's goal of a competitive, knowledge-driven economy (Kenya Vision 2030, 2007). Gifted education cultivates critical thinking, creativity, and problem-solving, crucial for economic growth and technological advancement. Moreover, it supports social equity by ensuring gifted students from diverse backgrounds have opportunities to excel, supporting Vision 2030's commitment to inclusive development. It also helps reduce gender disparities by identifying and nurturing talent among girls and marginalized groups, promoting broader societal equity goals (Kenya Vision 2030, 2007). In sum, gifted education would foster a skilled, innovative, and inclusive workforce essential for Kenya's growth.

Methods Used by Teachers in Identifying Giftedness

The definition of giftedness varies across contexts but generally refers to individuals with exceptional abilities in intellectual, creative, artistic, or leadership domains. In Kenya, the identification of giftedness is still evolving, with most educational institutions relying on classroom performance and teacher observation to recognize gifted students (Ndirangu et al., 2007). Teachers often use informal methods, such as self-developed tests, classroom observations, and teacher recommendations, to identify gifted students. Studies indicate that 96.7% of teachers use self-prepared tests to assess potential giftedness, while only 13.1% use standardized IQ tests due to limited access to these, and resources for formal assessment (Bundotich & Kimaiyo, 2015).

Teachers may observe specific behaviors such as advanced reasoning, independent problem-solving, or deep curiosity, aligning with characteristics described in Piaget’s theory of cognitive development. However, awareness of the unique needs and behaviors of gifted learners varies, as most teachers lack specialized training in identifying and nurturing these students (Ngigi & Ndurumo, 2007).

Internationally, gifted education relies on a broader and more structured process, often including standardized tests, psychometric assessments, and teacher nominations. For example, in the United States, tools such as the Stanford-Binet IQ test and the SAT are used to identify gifted students (Wormald, 2017). In South Korea, gifted students are identified through multiple criteria, including national standardized tests and teacher nominations (Ogurlu, 2016). The reliance on informal methods and teacher perceptions underscores the need for better training and structured support systems to identify and foster gifted learners in Kenya's public schools. Current methods are insufficient to capture the diverse manifestations of giftedness, such as cognitive, artistic, or leadership abilities (Loveless, 2024). This gap likely leads to inconsistent recognition and support, with many gifted students remaining unidentified due to a lack of formal identification processes.

CBC and Specialized Programs for Gifted Learners

The Competency-Based Curriculum (CBC), introduced in Kenya in 2017, aims to cater to diverse learner abilities by emphasizing skills, creativity, and individualized learning. While CBC provides a more flexible, learner-centered approach than the previous 8-4-4 system, it may not fully replace the need for specialized programs specifically designed for gifted learners.

The CBC encourages differentiation within classrooms by allowing teachers to design learning activities based on students' abilities and interests. This structure can benefit gifted students by providing opportunities for more advanced, hands-on, and personalized learning experiences. However, research suggests that without targeted programs or dedicated resources, general classroom differentiation may not adequately address the needs of gifted learners who require significantly more challenging and accelerated content than what is typically offered (Dinnocenti, 1998).

While CBC encourages projects and problem-solving skills that could engage gifted learners, teachers often lack the training and resources to sufficiently challenge them. Many teachers in Kenya have expressed difficulties in implementing the CBC due to large class sizes, limited resources, and the need for specific training on advanced pedagogical strategies. Consequently, gifted students may still require specialized programs or acceleration options that CBC alone may not provide (Cheptanui, 2011).

Furthermore, experts argue that a specialized approach, such as dedicated gifted programs, provides the gifted learners with opportunities for intellectual peer interaction, which is essential for their social and emotional development. Without specialized programs, gifted learners may struggle with boredom, underachievement, or lack of motivation due to insufficient academic challenges. For these reasons, while CBC offers a more adaptable framework, it should be complemented by specialized programs, enrichment, and teacher training to effectively meet the unique needs of gifted learners in Kenya (Olszewski-Kubilius & Thomson, 2012).

Many countries around the world have established comprehensive policies to support gifted education, acknowledging the distinct needs of gifted learners and the necessity of providing them with appropriate educational opportunities. For example, in the United States, the Jacob K. Javits Gifted and Talented Students Education Act (the Javits Act) allocates federal resources specifically for gifted programs, ensuring that students, including those from disadvantaged backgrounds, have access to specialized support for their advanced learning needs (Wormald, 2017). Such programs not only promote academic success but also contribute to the social and emotional growth of gifted learners by encouraging interaction with like-minded peers.

In contrast, Kenya's approach to gifted education is less developed and lacks a designated funding stream for gifted programs, which limits the creation of initiatives that could support gifted students from various socio-economic backgrounds. While the Competency-Based Curriculum (CBC) has made education more flexible, it does not specifically cater to the needs of gifted students without additional support systems (Mwangasha et al., 2019). As a result, many gifted learners in Kenya face challenges such as a lack of stimulation and disengagement, which can lead to underachievement and boredom (Ogoda, 2000).

The Role of the Private Sector in Gifted Education

The private sector has played an important role in gifted education across various countries, with a focus on funding, curriculum development, and supplementary programs that can enhance access to specialized resources for gifted students. Kenya could learn from these examples to develop and implement effective gifted education programs.

1. **Funding and Sponsorships**

In the United States, the private sector has been instrumental in funding gifted programs. Organizations like the Davidson Institute provide scholarships, grants, and resources specifically for gifted students, supporting their educational journey with both financial and developmental resources. Private foundations and corporations have invested in programs that provide enrichment opportunities, competitions, and specialized curricula, which public schools might not have the resources to offer (Davidson Institute, 2023). Kenya can learn from this by encouraging corporate social responsibility (CSR) initiatives that sponsor gifted education programs, particularly in areas with limited public funding, such as the *Wings to Fly* program of Equity Bank, which may be expanded into a gifted learners' initiative.

2. **Partnerships with Educational Institutions**

In Singapore, the private sector collaborates closely with the Ministry of Education to provide specialized programs, such as those offered through the Gifted Education Programme (GEP). Singapore's GEP is supported by partnerships with private educational consultants and institutions, helping the program remain adaptable to changing educational needs and advances. Private companies also sponsor technology and resources, enabling a more tailored and intensive learning experience (Singapore Ministry of Education, 2018). For Kenya, partnering with private firms could provide public schools access to resources like digital tools, labs, and mentorship programs that could foster the growth of gifted learners.

3. **Teacher Training and Curriculum Development**

In Australia, private sector involvement in gifted education includes funding teacher training in identifying and nurturing gifted students. Private foundations often sponsor workshops, conferences, and certifications for teachers to equip them with skills necessary for differentiated instruction for gifted students (Gross, 2019). Kenya could adopt similar initiatives by collaborating with private organizations to sponsor teacher training programs, which could improve the identification and support of gifted learners within the mainstream education system.

4. **Establishing Specialized Institutions and Programs**

Private institutions in India, such as the NIIT Foundation, have focused on specialized programs for gifted students, particularly in technology and STEM fields. These programs offer advanced coursework, mentorship, and real-world applications for gifted learners, creating pathways into higher education and the workforce for highly talented students (NIIT Foundation, 2022). For Kenya, establishing private sector-led initiatives or schools dedicated to gifted education could provide a structured environment where gifted students can flourish outside of the conventional schooling system.

Legal Framework Supporting Gifted Education

Currently, Kenya lacks a comprehensive legal framework dedicated to the implementation of gifted education. While educational policies such as the Basic Education Act (2013) emphasize inclusive education, there is limited specific legislative guidance focused on gifted learners' unique needs. This lack of a targeted framework hinders the structured identification, development, and support of gifted students. Specifically, the following work against the success of gifted education:

1. **Absence of Specific Legislation for Gifted Education**
Kenyan educational policy frameworks, including Kenya Vision 2030 and the Competency-Based Curriculum (CBC), emphasize equity and quality in education but do not specifically address gifted education (Republic of Kenya, 2007; Kenya Institute of Curriculum Development, 2017). Unlike other countries that have detailed legislative provisions for gifted learners, Kenya's general policies lack provisions tailored for gifted education. This gap affects the formal recognition and support for gifted students, limiting access to specialized resources, teacher training, and differentiated programs (Wambugu & Kibui, 2019).

2. **Inclusive Education Policies Do Not Address Gifted Needs**
Kenya's current approach to inclusive education focuses primarily on students with disabilities and those from marginalized communities, aiming to bridge the gap in access for these groups. However, the needs of gifted learners, who require a more advanced curriculum and faster-paced instruction, are not explicitly covered. Without a clear mandate or framework, schools and teachers often lack the legal backing or incentives to identify and develop these learners' abilities (Njenga & Mwangi, 2020). This oversight limits

opportunities for gifted students and underscores the need for legislative reform to support them.

3. **The Role of Policy Gaps in Teacher Training and Resources**
In the absence of a legal framework, there are also gaps in teacher training and resource allocation for gifted education. Teachers in Kenya are not formally trained to identify and support gifted students, as the Teacher Service Commission does not mandate specialized training or resources for gifted education. Studies indicate that teachers often lack both the skills and resources to differentiate instruction for high-ability students, further emphasizing the need for legislation that addresses these issues directly (Muthee & Sang, 2017).

4. **Comparative Models**
Countries such as the United States, Singapore, and South Korea have established legal provisions or policies for gifted education, ensuring that gifted students receive adequate support in curriculum, identification, and assessment. These frameworks mandate specialized teacher training, advanced curricula, and supportive resources tailored for gifted learners (Passow, 2018). By adopting similar legislation, Kenya could ensure structured and consistent support for gifted students nationwide.

Conclusion

In conclusion, the necessity for a robust framework for gifted education in Kenya is paramount. The current educational system inadequately supports gifted learners, risking the loss of potential innovators and leaders, essential for national development. Prominent examples of gifted individuals, such as Calestous Juma and Nora Okong'o, illustrate the profound impact that nurturing this talent can have on society. Despite policy recommendations advocating for improved identification and support mechanisms, progress has been slow, leaving many gifted students, such as Elias Muthomi Gitonga, unrecognized and unsupported. To align with Kenya's Vision 2030 goals, it is crucial to enhance teacher training, implement specialized assessment tools, and develop structured programs tailored to meet the needs of gifted learners. Such initiatives will not only foster a skilled workforce but also promote social equity by ensuring that all talented students, regardless of their background, have access to opportunities that cultivate their abilities. Addressing these challenges will be vital for Kenya's socio-economic advancement and global competitiveness.

References

1. Bundotich, J., & Kimaiyo, J. (2015). Assessment of teacher awareness of gifted children and resource availability for their learning in regular public primary schools of Mwatate Sub-County, Kenya.
2. Cheptanui, S. M. (2011). Instructional strategies of educating learners identified by teachers as gifted and talented in primary schools in Wareng District, Kenya.
3. Davidson Institute. (2023). *Gifted education programs and resources.* Retrieved from https://www.davidsongifted.org
4. Dinnocenti, S. T. (1998). Differentiation: Definition and description for gifted and talented. National Research Center on the Gifted and Talented.
5. Gross, M. (2019). Teacher training for the gifted: A review of best practices. *Australasian Journal of Gifted Education, 28*(1), 7–16.
6. Lisumba, D. (2022, December 5). Kenyan boy Elias Muthomi Gitonga honored among global gifted children. *The Daily Nation.*
7. Loveless, T. (2024). *The diverse dimensions of giftedness: Exploring cognitive and creative potentials.* London: Academic Press.
8. Luvinzu, P. (2021). The future of gifted education in Africa. *Journal of Advanced Educational Research, 15*(3), 250–265.
9. Kang'ethe, R., & Karugu, G. (1995). A study of gifted learners in Kenyan primary schools. *Kenya Journal of Educational Studies, 12*(3), 78–84.
10. Kenya Institute of Curriculum Development. (2017). Basic education curriculum framework.
11. Matilda, J., Kariuki, P., & Omulema, B. (2019). Challenges facing gifted education in Kenyan public schools. *Journal of Educational Studies, 10*(1), 56–69.
12. Muthee, J., & Sang, T. (2017). Teacher training and gifted education in Kenya: A gap analysis. *International Journal of Teacher Education, 5*(2), 23–31.
13. Mwangasha, E., Wambua, T., & Kibe, L. (2019). Implementation of CBC in Kenya: Implications for gifted learners. *Educational Policy Review, 8*(4), 98–107.

14. Njenga, P., & Mwangi, G. (2020). Challenges facing inclusive education in Kenya: A focus on policy and legal framework. *Journal of Education and Social Sciences, 6*(1), 12-20.
15. Ndirangu, M., Mwangi, P., & Changeiywo, J. (2007). Educational provision for the academically gifted in Kenya: Rhetoric or reality: Case of primary schools in Nyandarua District, Kenya. *Eastern African Social Science Research Review, 23*(2), 55-69.
16. Ngigi, M., & Ndurumo, M. (2007). Teacher perceptions of giftedness in Kenya. *Kenya Educational Review, 9*(1), 34–47.
17. NIIT Foundation. (2022). NIIT Foundation and Angel One partner to uplift underserved youth. Retrieved from https://www.dqindia.com/news/niit-foundation-and-angel-one-partner-to-uplift-underserved-youth-4795744
18. Nordling, L. (2017, December 19). Calestous Juma: Scholar who bridged Africa's development gaps. *Nature.* https://doi.org/10.1038/d41586-017-08836-3
19. Ogoda, A. (2000). Identification of gifted and talented learners with hearing impairment in inclusive education.
20. Ogurlu, U. (2016). The importance of gifted individuals for society. *Journal of Gifted Education.*
21. Olszewski-Kubilius, P., & Thomson, D. (2012). Gifted children and peer relationships. In *Gifted education: Current perspectives and future directions* (pp. 45-66).
22. Passow, A. H. (2018). Influence of gifted instructional strategies on gifted children's learning outcomes [Doctoral dissertation, Liberty University]. Liberty University Digital Commons.
https://digitalcommons.liberty.edu/cgi/viewcontent.cgi?article=5895&context=doctoral
23. Republic of Kenya. (2007). Kenya Vision 2030. Government of Kenya.
24. Republic of Kenya. (2012). Sessional Paper No. 14 on education and training reform. Government Printer.
25. Republic of Kenya. (2013). Basic Education Act 2013. Government Printer.
26. Reid, A., & Horváthová, B. (2020). Specialized teacher training for gifted education. *European Journal of Teacher Education.*
27. Shavinina, L. V. (2019). On giftedness and economy: The impact of talented individuals on the global economy. In L. V. Shavinina (Ed.),

International handbook on giftedness (pp. 883–894). Springer. https://doi.org/10.1007/978-1-4020-6162-2_47

28. Singapore Ministry of Education. (2018). MOE FY2018 Committee of Supply Debate Response by Minister for Education (Schools), Mr Ng Chee Meng. Retrieved from https://www.moe.gov.sg/news/speeches/20180305-moe-fy2018-committee-of-supply-debate-response-by-minister-for-education-schools-mr-ng-chee-meng
29. USAID. (2023). *Youth empowerment and entrepreneurship: Supporting Africa's future innovators*. Retrieved from https://www.usaid.gov
30. Wambugu, E., & Kibui, K. (2019). Inclusive education and gifted learners in Kenya. *Journal of Inclusive Education, 11*(4), 245–261.
31. Wormald, T. (2017). Policies and practices in gifted education: A global perspective. *Gifted Education International, 33*(1), 5–15

Chapter 2

Provision of Early Childhood Education in Kenya

Early Childhood Education (ECE) in Kenya has undergone substantial changes over time, evolving from traditional teaching methods that emphasized social integration and cultural value transmission, to a more structured approach. This formalization started in the 1970s, driven by a growing understanding of how early learning impacts children's cognitive, social, and emotional growth (Kakande, 2019). The early years are essential as they establish the groundwork for future success, helping children develop crucial skills, attitudes, and concepts. During this period, children acquire language, perceptual and motor skills, which aid in reading and writing, as well as basic numeracy, problem-solving abilities, a love for learning, and interpersonal skills (Government of Uganda, 2005).

Recent statistics from the Kenya National Bureau of Statistics (KNBS) reveal encouraging trends in enrolment at the pre-primary level. In 2022, enrolment rates in ECE institutions reached approximately 92% of eligible children aged 3 to 6 years (KNBS, 2022). This reflects a significant increase from previous years, indicating a growing realization among parents that early childhood education has an important influence on their children's learning later in life. Additionally, the government has implemented policies to enhance the quality of ECE, such as the National ECE Policy 2019, which outlines standards for curriculum, teacher training, and the learning environment (Ministry of Education, 2019).

Globally, Early Childhood Education (ECE) is recognized as important within the Sustainable Development Goals (SDGs), particularly in Goal 4, which seeks to guarantee inclusive and equitable quality education for all, starting from early childhood. SDG 4 highlights the necessity of providing access to quality pre-primary education to ensure that all children are prepared for primary school education (UNESCO, 2015). In Kenya, aligning national ECE policies with global education goals is critical for fostering an inclusive educational environment that promotes lifelong learning opportunities for all. This commitment to early childhood education is crucial for reducing educational disparities and ensuring that all children, regardless of socio-economic status, have the chance to succeed in a nurturing learning environment.

Importance of Early Childhood Education

Early Childhood Education (ECE) is critical for the holistic development of children and lays the foundation for lifelong learning and well-being. Several reasons highlight its importance:

• ECE programs stimulate children's cognitive development through structured play and learning activities. Research indicates that high-quality ECE enhances language skills, critical thinking, and problem-solving abilities, leading to better academic performance in later years (Barnett, 2011).

• Early childhood education fosters social and emotional skills, including cooperation, empathy, and self-regulation. Children learn to interact with peers, manage emotions, and build relationships, which are essential for success in school and life (Denham et al., 2012).

• Participation in ECE prepares children for the transition to primary school education. It equips them with foundational skills such as literacy, numeracy, and the ability to follow instructions, ultimately leading to increased school readiness and reduced dropout rates (McCoy et al., 2017).

• ECE programs provide equal opportunities for all children, regardless of socio-economic status. Access to quality early education helps bridge the gap for disadvantaged children, ensuring that they enter primary school with the necessary skills and knowledge to succeed (Heckman, 2006).

• Investing in early childhood education yields significant economic returns. Studies show that resources spent result in economic benefits through reduced needs for remedial education, lower crime rates, and increased productivity (Heckman, 2006).

• ECE programs often engage families, providing them with resources and support that enhance child development. This involvement fosters a home environment conducive to learning and strengthens the relationship between parents and children (Baker et al., 2016).

• ECE cultivates a love for learning in children. By introducing them to diverse experiences and knowledge at an early age, ECE encourages curiosity and intrinsic motivation, setting the stage for lifelong learning (Whitebread et al., 2017).

Stakeholders in the Provision of Early Childhood Education in Kenya

Effective provision of early childhood education involves the active participation of various stakeholders. These stakeholders range from the government to non-governmental organizations, the private sector, local communities, and parents. Each of these actors has a unique role to play, contributing to the availability, quality, and sustainability of ECE services.

The government is one of the most significant stakeholders in the provision of early childhood education. It formulates policy frameworks, regulatory functions, and provides funding to ensure that ECE programs are accessible and meet the required standards. The 2010 Constitution devolved the responsibility of managing ECE services to county governments, giving them the mandate to manage the recruitment of teachers, develop infrastructure, and ensure the quality of ECE programs (Republic of Kenya, 2010).

The Ministry of Education (MoE) provides guidelines and policies that regulate the development of the ECE curriculum and the training of ECE teachers. The Kenya Institute of Curriculum Development (KICD) has developed the Competency-Based Curriculum (CBC), which includes a comprehensive ECE component (KICD, 2017). The government's involvement extends to monitoring and evaluation through the Teachers Service Commission (TSC) to ensure that qualified teachers are recruited and that ECE centers are adequately supervised.

However, challenges persist in government funding. Although the Free Primary Education (FPE) initiative was introduced in 2003, it did not extend to ECE, leaving parents to bear the costs of early childhood education (Ng'asike, 2019). County governments also face financial constraints, leading to disparities in the quality of ECE services across different regions.

Non-governmental organizations (NGOs) are another stakeholder that plays a crucial role in filling the gaps left by the government, especially in underserved areas. Organizations such as Plan International, UNICEF, and World Vision have been active in advocating for and supporting ECE programs across Kenya. UNICEF, for example, has supported the Kenyan government in developing policies and strategies to improve the quality of ECE through funding and technical assistance (UNICEF, 2014). NGOs also engage in advocacy, promoting inclusive education for children with disabilities, ensuring that marginalized communities have access to ECE, and enhancing teacher training programs.

Moreover, NGOs have introduced innovative teaching and learning methods, such as the use of technology and child-centered approaches in ECE centers. In collaboration with other partners, they have provided learning materials and established model learning centers that serve as benchmarks for quality ECE provision in the country (Mweru, 2020).

Despite their significant contributions, the involvement of NGOs in the provision of ECE is often limited to specific regions or short-term projects. This creates a challenge in achieving sustainability and uniformity across the country, with some areas benefiting more than others.

The private sector, on the other hand, includes private schools and corporate entities. This is another important stakeholder in the provision of ECE in Kenya. Private ECE centers have increased significantly over the past two decades, especially in urban areas where parents are willing and able to pay for quality services (Makoti, 2011). These centers often offer better infrastructure, a more favorable teacher-student ratio, and a wider range of learning materials compared to public ECE centers.

Private companies also contribute to ECE through corporate social responsibility (CSR) programs. For instance, Safaricom Foundation and Equity Group Foundation have invested in the development of early childhood infrastructure and digital learning tools for ECE learners (Safaricom Foundation, 2022). Through these initiatives, private companies have improved access to quality education for many children, particularly in low-income areas.

However, the growth of private ECE centers has raised concerns about equity in education. The commercialization of early childhood education has led to disparities, with children from affluent backgrounds accessing high-quality education, while those from poor families are often left to contend with under-resourced public centers. This trend has the potential to exacerbate inequality in educational outcomes (Sifuna, 2020).

Parents and guardians are central stakeholders in the provision of early childhood education. As the primary caregivers, parents play a vital role in the cognitive, emotional, and social development of children during the early years. Parental involvement in ECE is not only through the payment of fees but also through active participation in school activities, supporting learning at home, and ensuring regular attendance of their children at school.

The role of parents in ECE has been emphasized in Kenya's Basic Education Act (2013), which encourages parental participation in the management of schools. Research shows that when parents are actively involved in their children's education, there is an improvement in academic performance, behavior, and school attendance (Ogunyemi, 2017).

However, in low-income areas, parents may struggle to support their children's early education due to financial constraints, lack of awareness, or competing priorities such as livelihood activities. This affects not only their ability to pay school fees but also their involvement in their children's learning (Ng'asike, 2019).

Local communities are important actors in the provision of early childhood education in Kenya. In rural areas, communities have traditionally provided support for the construction and maintenance of ECE centers, often through Harambee (self-help) initiatives. Community-based organizations (CBOs) and faith-based organizations (FBOs) also contribute by mobilizing resources and sensitizing parents on the importance of early childhood education (Kameri-Mbote, 2018).

Local communities often collaborate with NGOs and local governments to implement ECE programs. In some cases, community members provide in-kind support by offering land for the construction of ECE centers, donating materials, or volunteering their time as caregivers. Such involvement helps to ensure that ECE services are tailored to the cultural and social needs of the community, which is essential for the holistic development of young learners.

However, community involvement can be inconsistent, particularly in urban areas where traditional communal ties are weaker. Additionally, in some rural areas, communities lack the financial capacity to support ECE services effectively, leading to poorly equipped centers and underqualified teachers (Munywoki, 2016).

As can be seen, the provision of early childhood education in Kenya is a multifaceted endeavor that requires the active involvement of various stakeholders. The government plays a central role in setting policies and standards, but its capacity to deliver quality ECE services is often constrained by financial and administrative challenges. NGOs, the private sector, parents, and local communities all make significant contributions, each bringing their unique strengths and resources to the table. However, the uneven involvement of these stakeholders, particularly in terms of geographic and socioeconomic disparities, presents a major challenge to achieving universal access to quality ECE in Kenya. Moving forward, there is a need for stronger collaboration and coordination among all stakeholders to ensure that early childhood education is accessible, equitable, and of high quality across the country.

Challenges Facing Early Childhood Education in Kenya

Despite significant strides made in enhancing Early Childhood Education (ECE), several challenges persist that hinder its effectiveness and accessibility. These challenges encompass various dimensions, including infrastructure, quality of education, teacher training, and socio-economic factors. Below are some of the key challenges facing ECE in Kenya:

1. **Inadequate Infrastructure and Resources**
   Many ECE centers in Kenya lack adequate infrastructure and learning resources. A significant number of schools operate in poorly constructed facilities that are not conducive to learning. According to a report by the Kenya National Bureau of Statistics (KNBS) (2021), over 60% of ECE centers do not meet the minimum infrastructure standards, which impacts the overall learning environment for children. Additionally, there is a shortage of essential learning materials, such as books and educational toys, which are critical for interactive and play-based learning.

2. **Shortage of Qualified Teachers**
   The quality of ECE largely depends on the training and qualifications of educators. There is a significant shortage of qualified ECE teachers, particularly in rural and underserved areas. Many teachers lack formal training in early childhood education, which affects the quality of instruction and care provided to children (Ng'ang'a, 2018). A study by the World Bank (2019) highlighted that only 30% of ECE teachers in Kenya possess the required qualifications, leading to concerns about the effectiveness of educational delivery.

3. **Lack of Standardization and Quality Assurance**
There is an absence of standardized guidelines for ECE curricula and quality assurance mechanisms in many regions. While the Kenyan government has developed policies to promote quality ECE, implementation remains inconsistent. The lack of monitoring and evaluation systems makes it challenging to ensure adherence to quality standards across ECE centers (Kakande, 2019). This inconsistency can lead to varying educational experiences for children, depending on the region and resources available.

4. **Socio-Economic Barriers**
Socio-economic factors play a significant role in access to quality ECE in Kenya. Many families, especially in low-income and rural areas, cannot afford the fees associated with ECE, despite the government's efforts to provide free or subsidized education. According to a study by the United Nations Children's Fund (UNICEF) (2020), approximately 30% of children aged 3 to 6 years are not enrolled in any form of ECE, primarily due to financial constraints (UNICEF, 2020). This lack of access perpetuates cycles of poverty and educational inequality.

5. **Inadequate Parental Engagement**
Parental involvement is crucial for children's learning and development. However, many parents in Kenya are either unaware of the importance of ECE or lack the capacity to engage meaningfully in their children's education. A study by Mugambi (2020) found that low levels of parental involvement negatively impacts children's educational outcomes, highlighting the need for more community awareness and engagement initiatives.

6. **Cultural Beliefs and Attitudes**
Cultural perceptions on education can also pose challenges to ECE in Kenya. In some communities, there is a preference for informal or traditional forms of education over formal ECE. These cultural beliefs may discourage families from enrolling their children in ECE programs, leading to lower participation rates (Kinyanjui, 2018). Addressing these attitudes requires targeted awareness campaigns that highlight the benefits of quality early childhood education.

While the Kenyan government has made significant strides in promoting Early Childhood Education, several challenges persist that undermine its effectiveness and accessibility. Addressing these challenges requires a multifaceted approach that includes improving infrastructure and increasing funding.

Diversity of Stakeholders and Quality Challenges in ECE

The provision of Early Childhood Education (ECE) in Kenya is a collaborative effort involving multiple stakeholders, such as the government, non-governmental organizations (NGOs), the private sector, local communities, and parents. While these stakeholders play crucial roles in the development and delivery of ECE services, the involvement of multiple actors presents several quality-related challenges. These challenges stem from issues such as disparities in resources, inconsistent standards, teacher qualification concerns, infrastructure limitations, and governance gaps. The following are some of the quality challenges that exist in ECE due to the involvement of diverse players:

1. **Inconsistent Funding and Resource Allocation**
   One of the most significant quality challenges is the inconsistency in funding and resource allocation. The Kenyan government, through county governments, is responsible for managing public ECE centers; however, the level of funding varies significantly from one county to another. Some counties prioritize ECE in their budgets, while others allocate limited resources, leading to disparities in the quality of services provided (Ng'asike, 2019).

Additionally, the absence of national funding mechanisms comparable to the Free Primary Education (FPE) initiative means that ECE remains largely dependent on parental contributions, which can vary based on socioeconomic status. This results in some centers being under-resourced, with inadequate learning materials, furniture, or even proper sanitation facilities. NGOs and the private sector provide additional support, but their contributions are often project-based and geographically targeted, meaning that only certain areas benefit. While some regions see improved ECE infrastructure and access to resources due to NGO interventions, others lag behind, creating inequities in the quality of education provided across different regions.

2. **Disparities in Teacher Training and Qualification**
   Teacher quality is a crucial determinant of the overall quality of ECE. However, Kenya faces challenges related to the training, qualification, and

professional development of ECE teachers. The Teachers Service Commission (TSC) sets qualifications for ECE teachers, but there is significant variation in teacher training, particularly between public and private ECE centers (Mweru, 2020).

In some cases, private centers employ underqualified or untrained teachers to minimize costs. This often leads to poor teaching practices that do not align with the curriculum or best practices in early childhood education. However, some private centers, especially high-end institutions, invest in well-trained teachers, creating a gap in teaching quality between affluent and low-income regions. Government efforts to regulate teacher training and employment are often limited by financial and logistical constraints. Furthermore, since counties are responsible for recruiting and paying ECE teachers, disparities arise between counties based on their ability to offer competitive salaries, which affects teacher retention and motivation.

3. **Infrastructure and Learning Environment Challenges**
The learning environment, including classroom infrastructure, is another area where quality challenges are evident. While some private and NGO-supported centers boast modern classrooms with child-friendly facilities, many public and community-based ECE centers lack basic infrastructure (Makoti, 2011). Poor classroom conditions, overcrowding, and inadequate learning materials are common challenges in underfunded public ECE centers.

Rural and marginalized areas are particularly affected by poor infrastructure, which hinders the ability of children to learn in a conducive environment. For example, some ECE centers operate in temporary structures or under trees, exposing learners to harsh weather conditions. The absence of adequate playgrounds and recreational facilities further limits holistic child development, which is essential at the ECE stage. Efforts by local communities and county governments to improve infrastructure are often insufficient due to budgetary limitations. NGOs occasionally step in to bridge the gap, but their involvement is not always sustained, and their interventions may not cover all affected areas, leading to regional inequalities.

4. **Curriculum Implementation and Adaptation Challenges**
The introduction of Kenya's Competency-Based Curriculum (CBC), which includes ECE, is an important step toward improving the quality of education.

However, its implementation presents challenges due to the uneven capacity of different stakeholders to adapt to the new curriculum (KICD, 2017).

Teachers in under-resourced public and community-based centers often struggle to implement the CBC effectively because they lack adequate training and teaching materials. Private ECE centers, particularly those serving middle- and upper-income families, tend to be better equipped to implement the new curriculum, leading to variations in the quality of education provided. Furthermore, the adaptation of the CBC to suit local contexts, particularly in marginalized regions, remains a challenge, as these areas may not have the resources or teacher expertise to modify the curriculum in ways that reflect local cultures and environments.

NGOs and private actors have been instrumental in providing training and resources to improve curriculum implementation, but the reach of these interventions is often limited. The government's capacity to roll out the CBC uniformly across the country is constrained by logistical and financial hurdles, leading to inconsistent quality of education delivery.

5. **Governance and Coordination Issues**

The governance structure of ECE in Kenya is complex, with responsibilities shared between national and county governments, NGOs, the private sector, and local communities. This decentralization, while intended to bring decision-making closer to the people, has led to coordination challenges that affect the quality of ECE services.

For instance, the lack of clear communication and collaboration between county governments and national education authorities has resulted in gaps in teacher recruitment, resource allocation, and curriculum implementation (Munywoki, 2016). In some cases, ECE teachers are not paid on time, which affects their morale and the quality of teaching they provide.

Additionally, the involvement of NGOs and private entities in the provision of ECE, while beneficial in many respects, often leads to fragmented service delivery. Different actors may pursue their own priorities without sufficient alignment with national education policies, which can create discrepancies in how ECE services are provided across the country.

6. **Equity and Inclusion Challenges**
Equity in access to quality ECE services remains a critical challenge, especially for children from marginalized communities, including those in arid and semi-arid lands (ASALs), urban informal settlements, and children with disabilities. Despite efforts to promote inclusive education, many ECE centers are not adequately equipped to cater to the needs of children with disabilities or those from vulnerable backgrounds (Ogunyemi, 2017).

Private centers, often better resourced, may provide specialized services for children with disabilities, but these are typically unaffordable for many families. Public centers, on the other hand, frequently lack the necessary facilities or trained personnel to support inclusive education, leading to the exclusion of children with special needs. NGOs have made strides in promoting inclusive education by supporting teacher training and providing learning materials for children with disabilities, but these efforts are often limited in scope. A more coordinated approach between government and NGOs is needed to address the equity and inclusion challenges in ECE comprehensively.

While multiple stakeholders contribute to the provision of early childhood education in Kenya, their involvement introduces several quality challenges. These challenges include disparities in funding and resources, inconsistencies in teacher training, inadequate infrastructure, curriculum implementation difficulties, governance and coordination issues, and equity concerns. Tackling these concerns necessitates a more unified approach from all stakeholders and a greater commitment from the government to ensure that every child, regardless of their background, has access to quality early childhood education.

Conclusion

The importance of Early Childhood Education cannot be overstated. It is a vital investment in the future of children, communities, and nations. By prioritizing and enhancing ECE, we can ensure that every child has the opportunity to reach their full potential and contribute positively to society. In conclusion, while Kenya has made notable strides in the development of Early Childhood Education (ECE), significant challenges remain that hinder its effectiveness and accessibility. The impressive enrolment rates reflect an increasing recognition of the importance of ECE, yet disparities in infrastructure, teacher qualifications, and socio-economic barriers continue to affect the quality of education provided. The involvement of various stakeholders, including the government, NGOs, the private sector, parents, and local communities, is crucial for addressing these challenges. However, inconsistent funding, inadequate resources, and governance issues complicate efforts to ensure equitable access to quality ECE for all children. To foster a more inclusive and effective ECE system, a coordinated approach that prioritizes collaboration among stakeholders, alongside sustained government support and investment, is essential. By addressing these challenges, Kenya can enhance the educational landscape for its youngest learners, ultimately promoting lifelong learning and reducing educational inequalities.

References

1. Baker, J., Rieger, K., & Heller, S. (2016). Family engagement in early childhood education: A resource for practitioners. *Early Childhood Education Journal*, 44(2), 123-130.
2. Barnett, W. S. (2011). Effectiveness of early educational intervention. *Science*, 333(6045), 975-978.
3. Denham, S. A., Brown, C., & Domitrovich, C. (2012). The importance of social-emotional learning in early childhood education. *Early Childhood Research Quarterly*, 27(1), 1-3.
4. Government of Uganda. (2005). *Early childhood development policy*. Kampala: Ministry of Gender, Labour and Social Development.
5. Heckman, J. J. (2006). Skill formation and the economics of investing in disadvantaged children. *Science*, 312(5782), 1900-1902.
6. Kakande, M. (2019). The evolution of early childhood education in Kenya: Historical perspectives and current trends. *Journal of Education and Practice*, 10(12), 45-52.
7. Kameri-Mbote, P. (2018). Community involvement in early childhood education in Kenya: A socio-cultural perspective. *International Journal of Educational Development*, 61, 1-8.
8. Kenya Institute of Curriculum Development (KICD). (2017). *Competency-based curriculum for early childhood education*. Nairobi: KICD.
9. Kenya National Bureau of Statistics (KNBS). (2021). *Statistical abstract*. Nairobi: KNBS.

10. Kenya National Bureau of Statistics (KNBS). (2022). *Economic survey*. Nairobi: KNBS.
11. Makoti, N. (2011). The role of private sector in early childhood education in Kenya: Opportunities and challenges. *African Journal of Educational Studies*, 7(1), 15-24.
12. Ministry of Education. (2019). *National ECE Policy*. Nairobi: Government Printer.
13. Mugambi, M. (2020). Parental involvement in early childhood education in Kenya: Challenges and opportunities. *Journal of Early Childhood Research*, 18(3), 239-252.
14. Mweru, A. (2020). The role of non-governmental organizations in enhancing early childhood education in Kenya: A case study approach. *International Journal of Child Care and Education Policy*, 14(1), 35-50.
15. Ng'asike, J. (2019). Financing early childhood education in Kenya: An analysis of the challenges and opportunities for sustainable funding models. *International Journal of Educational Management*, 33(6), 1125-1138.
16. Ng'ang'a, R. (2018). Teacher training and professional development in early childhood education in Kenya: Current trends and future directions. *Journal of Education Policy*, 33(4), 487-502.
17. Ogunyemi, B. (2017). The impact of parental involvement on children's educational outcomes in low-income communities in Kenya: A qualitative study. *Childhood Education*, 93(3), 205-212.
18. Republic of Kenya. (2010). *The Constitution of Kenya*. Nairobi: Government Printer.
19. Safaricom Foundation. (2022). Investing in education: Safaricom Foundation's initiatives to support early childhood education in Kenya [Press release]. Nairobi: Safaricom Foundation.
20. Sifuna, D.N. (2020). The commercialization of early childhood education in Kenya: Implications for equity and access to quality education for all children. *Educational Research for Policy and Practice*, 19(3), 215-228.
21. UNESCO. (2015). *Education for all 2000-2015: Achievements and challenges*. Paris: UNESCO Publishing.
22. UNICEF (2014). Supporting the government of Kenya to improve the quality of early childhood education [Report]. Nairobi: UNICEF Kenya Country Office.
23. UNICEF (2020). The state of the world's children 2020: Children's rights and the COVID-19 pandemic [Report]. New York: UNICEF.

24. Whitebread, D., Coltman, P., Jameson, H., & Lander, R. (2017). The development of two observational tools for assessing preschool children's self-regulation and social-emotional skills: A pilot study with implications for practice and policy. *International Journal of Child Care and Education Policy*, 11(1), 1-18.
25. World Bank Group (2019). The state of the teaching profession in Kenya: An analysis of teacher qualifications and training needs across early childhood education centers [Report]. Washington DC: World Bank Group.

Chapter 3

Physical Facility Challenges Facing Kenyan Public Universities in Provision of Quality Education

University education is a pivotal driver of socio-economic growth, individual empowerment, and national development. It plays a crucial role in preparing individuals to become knowledgeable citizens and effective contributors to the workforce. Globally, university education contributes significantly to the economic and social well-being of nations. Studies show that university graduates have higher income levels, lower unemployment rates, and greater job security compared to non-graduates (Bloom, Canning, & Chan, 2006). University education encourages critical thinking, innovation, and the acquisition of specialized skills, all of which are essential for competing in a globalized economy. Furthermore, universities serve as hubs of research and innovation, tackling complex issues such as climate change, healthcare, and digital transformation. This research fosters knowledge transfer between academia and industry, leading to advancements that benefit societies at large (Altbach, Reisberg, & Rumbley, 2009).

In Africa, higher education has long been recognized as a fundamental ingredient for spurring development and progress. According to the World Bank (2010), university education enhances human capital, which is essential for advancing the economic development of African nations. University-educated citizens contribute to improved health outcomes, political stability, and community development, addressing many of Africa's unique challenges such as poverty, high unemployment rates, and food security. With Africa's youthful population, universities also play a crucial role in reducing their unemployment by equipping students with marketable skills. Technical skills combined with an understanding of Africa's specific needs can drive entrepreneurship and create jobs, reducing poverty levels. Further, African universities are increasingly focusing on research that addresses local problems such as drought-resistant crops, affordable healthcare, and sustainable development practices (Teferra & Altbach, 2004).

In Kenya, university education has been crucial to national development, shaping leaders and providing skilled professionals across various sectors, including healthcare, education, technology, and agriculture. As the Kenyan economy shifts toward becoming more knowledge-based, the role of universities becomes even more significant. University education has been a catalyst for socio-economic mobility, providing many young Kenyans—especially from disadvantaged backgrounds—with opportunities to improve their lives. Graduates are equipped to engage in the labor market and meet the demands of an increasingly competitive job environment (Oketch, 2003). Furthermore, universities are instrumental in promoting civic engagement and fostering national unity by bringing together students from diverse cultural backgrounds.

Additionally, Kenya's Vision 2030 emphasizes the role of higher education in transforming the country into a middle-income level economy through science, technology, and innovation. Kenyan universities have become centers for cutting-edge research in different fields through partnerships with international institutions contributing to the country's sustainable development goals (GoK, 2007).

However, the provision of quality education in Kenyan public universities is increasingly becoming a significant concern due to poor-quality infrastructure. The challenges faced by Kenyan public universities regarding physical facilities are multifaceted and deeply interconnected. While these institutions have made strides in advancing knowledge and research, they continue to face numerous challenges related to physical facilities. The state of infrastructure—including lecture halls, libraries, laboratories, and recreational facilities—profoundly impacts the educational experience and academic outcomes of students. According to Bloom Hills Schools,[1] the physical learning environment plays a crucial role in shaping students' educational experiences and learning outcomes. Investing in the physical infrastructure of public universities is not merely a matter of improving facilities; it is an investment in the future of the nation and its human capital development. Without significant reforms and targeted investment, Kenyan public universities risk falling behind in their mission to provide quality education that meets both national and global standards.

One of the foremost challenges faced by public universities in Kenya is the shortage of adequate lecture halls and classrooms. Many institutions operate with overcrowded classes which compromises the learning experience. In some cases,

[1] https://www.bloomfield.org/

the student-to-faculty ratio exceeds acceptable standards leading to diminished interaction between students and instructors (Ndirangu & Udoto, 2011). Overcrowded lecture halls hinder effective communication and engagement. Students may struggle to participate actively in discussions leading to a passive learning experience (Deslauriers, 2019). At the same time, this demand for limited classroom space forces universities to adopt irregular timetables including evening and weekend classes, which may not be suitable for all students. This places a strain on academic resources as well.

Libraries serve as critical resources for academic research and learning; however, many public universities in Kenya face challenges related to insufficient library facilities. Many libraries lack essential resources including textbooks, journals and digital resources (Wekesa et al., 2015). Consequently, students and faculty often struggle to access necessary research materials, which undermines their academic pursuits (Makhanu, 2023). This inadequacy of library facilities can lead to a lack of thorough research resulting in poorer academic performance and diminished quality of students' dissertations and theses.

Another concern centres on science and technology programs where laboratory facilities are indispensable. Many public universities in Kenya face major challenges regarding the quality and availability of laboratory facilities. Outdated equipment and insufficient supplies hinder students' hands-on learning experiences (Odeo, 2020). This limits the provision of quality authentic learning experiences for faculty and students which is crucial for their professions. The inability to conduct experiments and engage in practical applications can result in graduates who are less competitive in the job market (Okwach, 2018).

Student accommodation is another critical area where public universities in Kenya face challenges. Many lack sufficient hostels and quality living facilities for students; as a result, students are often forced to seek alternative accommodation off-campus which can be costly and less secure (Otieno, 2019). The struggle to secure safe and affordable accommodation can distract students from their studies leading to lower academic performance (Juma, 2018). Students who must live off-campus may face additional financial strain affecting their overall university experience (Makokha, 2020).

Recreational facilities are an essential element of a holistic educational experience; however many public universities in Kenya lack adequate sports facilities leisure areas and spaces for extracurricular activities. The absence of such facilities can lead to an unbalanced academic life for students (Kibera, 2017). Access to recreational facilities contributes to students' mental and physical well-being which are crucial for academic success (Nyabera, 2021). Participating in extracurricular activities enhances students' teamwork leadership and communication skills, which are vital for their future careers (Mokaya, 2019).

Even where physical facilities exist, the challenge of maintaining these infrastructures persists. Budget constraints often hinder timely repairs and renovations leading to deteriorating conditions (Abubakar & Murwa 2018). Maintenance culture plays a critical role in determining the quality and longevity of university facilities. In Kenyan universities, inadequate maintenance practices have had significant implications on usability, safety and functionality of infrastructure. The issue of maintenance culture—or lack thereof—has affected facility quality leading to decreased overall effectiveness of these institutions in delivering quality education.

Lack of a maintenance culture has resulted in degradation of learning environments; inadequate maintenance practices have led to a rapid dilapidation of lecture halls, laboratories, libraries and other essential learning spaces. According to recent studies, a significant proportion of university facilities in Kenya suffer from infrastructural neglect resulting in inadequate physical conditions (Njoroge, 2018). Facilities such as seating, lighting and ventilation, which directly affect students' comfort and concentration are often overlooked in maintenance schedules; this negatively impacts learning quality by reducing the conduciveness of learning environments.

Lack of a proactive maintenance culture has also compromised safety standards; many institutions are often reactive rather than proactive when it comes to facility repairs, addressing issues only after they become severe (Onyango 2020). This approach has led to a backlog of maintenance needs that not only degrade facilities but also create potential safety hazards. Inadequately maintained infrastructure such as crumbling buildings, broken windows, damaged or vandalized electrical wiring, poses risks to students and staff, affecting their health and safety.

Laboratories, ICT centers and libraries are essential resources for academic success; however due to lack of consistent maintenance culture, these facilities often experience frequent breakdowns and long periods of non-functionality. For instance, poorly maintained lab equipment and outdated technology hinder students' ability to gain practical skills affecting learning outcomes especially in STEM fields (Odhiambo & Khaemba 2021). ICT facilities crucial for accessing digital resources and supporting research often remain underutilized or non-functional due maintenance lapses; this affects students' ability to engage in modern learning practices, thus, limiting faculty members' productivity.

Kenyan universities often incur higher costs by adopting a reactive maintenance approach, typically more expensive in the long run compared to a proactive maintenance; when minor repairs are delayed, they often escalate into major issues requiring more extensive and costly interventions. For instance, lack of regular maintenance on buildings may eventually necessitate complete structural repairs, even reconstruction, which can be a significant financial burden (Njuguna 2019). This reactive approach further limits funds that could otherwise be directed toward other educational resources or expanding university facilities to accommodate growing student populations.

A neglected maintenance culture by the universities can significantly damage their reputation, particularly when attracting prospective students and establishing partnerships. Research underscores that universities globally compete not only on academic excellence but also on the quality of their facilities, which reflect the institutions' commitment to optimal learning environment (UNESCO 2017). Poorly maintained infrastructure—such as outdated or broken-down equipment, deteriorating buildings—suggest a lack of institutional priority for quality (Oketch 2016). This perception can deter local and international students seeking modern well-equipped environments, discourage potential partners and donors who may view the institutions as lacking in strategic focus and resource stability (Wekesa & Kihoro 2015).

Improvements and Policy Recommendations

To address twin challenges of inadequate poorly maintained physical facilities in Kenyan public universities, it is essential to focus both on strategic investment and sustainable management practices; overcoming these issues can enhance quality of teaching and learning as physical resources directly impact students' academic experience and outcomes (Adeyemi Uko-Aviomoh, 2004). Here are several strategies for achieving this:

Public-Private Partnerships (PPP)

One way that Kenyan universities can address facility deficits is through public-private partnerships (PPP); PPPs enable universities to access additional funding and technical expertise from the private sector, thus lessening dependence on limited government funds. Countries like Malaysia have effectively utilized PPPs to expand higher education facilities, leading to more modern campuses and enhanced infrastructure for students (Leong & Hamzah, 2019). Locally, Jomo Kenyatta University of Agriculture and Technology's partnership with various firms to build specialized labs and research centres, serves as a successful example (Kamau, 2015). Through PPPs universities could lease or build facilities tailored to their needs, without bearing the full cost upfront. This model allows shared responsibility in infrastructure development and is particularly beneficial in high-cost areas like laboratories, ICT centres and research hubs. The increased collaboration may also provide students and faculty with access to cutting-edge resources and industry networks that can enhance both learning and research opportunities.

Leveraging Technology E-Learning Facilities

Investing in e-learning facilities can alleviate pressure on physical spaces and address inadequacies in existing infrastructure. COVID-19 pandemic showed how effective virtual learning environments can be, when access to physical spaces is limited. Universities worldwide, including Kenya's University of Nairobi, have transitioned some programs online, reducing reliance on physical spaces (Nyerere, 2020); institutions should further develop e-learning platforms, and digital resources which are comparatively cost-effective and sustainable over time. Moreover, blended learning models combine online and in-person instruction to reduce the demand on physical spaces, allowing existing resources to serve more students with fewer structural changes (Adams 2020). This approach modernizes teaching methods meeting the expectations of an increasingly tech-savvy student population and aligning to global trends in higher education.

Implementing Regular Maintenance Programs

Addressing poorly maintained facilities requires more proactive management and maintenance programs. Regular preventive maintenance of physical infrastructure not only reduces future repair costs but also extends the lifespan of existing facilities. The World Bank emphasizes the importance of developing maintenance schedules to ensure sustainable facility quality, especially in developing nations where resources are limited (World Bank, 2017). By institutionalizing these, Kenyan universities could establish dedicated Facility Management Units (FMUs) tasked with routine inspections and preventive maintenance. These units could use facility management software to schedule and track activities, ensuring accountability and transparency.

Enhancing Funding for University Infrastructure

While public universities in Kenya largely depend on government funding, prioritizing funds for critical infrastructure and maintenance is essential. Increased government support can directly improve the physical learning environment and allow for better resources in high-demand areas like ICT, libraries, and lecture halls. Local studies indicate that inadequate government funding has strained the education sector in Kenya (Sifuna, 2014). Government allocations need to be more strategic, focusing on both constructing new facilities and sustaining existing ones through continuous maintenance.

A model to consider is South Africa's university funding framework, where government and universities have co-developed a campus infrastructure fund that universities access by proposing justified development plans. Adapting such a framework can ensure funds are directed toward priority projects that align with the long-term institutional goals and student needs.

Promoting Sustainable Building Practices

Sustainability is increasingly critical in managing educational facilities. Kenyan universities can adopt green building practices, such as using energy-efficient materials, harvesting rainwater, and utilizing solar energy, to reduce operational costs and environmental impact. Strathmore University in Kenya has implemented a solar power system, demonstrating its commitment to sustainable development and reducing costs in the long term. These practices not only align with global sustainability goals but also reduce dependency on unreliable utilities and creating a more conducive learning environment.

In conclusion, the role of university education in driving socio-economic development, particularly in Kenya, is undeniable. However, the challenges posed by inadequate and poorly maintained physical infrastructure in public universities hinder the potential of these institutions to provide quality education. Overcrowded classrooms, insufficient learning resources, outdated laboratories, and inadequate student accommodation limit academic engagement and outcomes. To address these challenges, it is crucial for universities to explore innovative solutions, such as public-private partnerships, investment in e-learning platforms, and proactive maintenance programs. Sustainable building practices and effective government funding allocation are also key to ensuring that infrastructure meets the growing demands of modern education. By adopting these strategies, Kenyan public universities can enhance their educational offerings, foster a conducive learning environment, and contribute more effectively to national development goals. Ultimately, these efforts will ensure that universities continue to shape skilled, empowered graduates who can drive both local and global progress.

References

1. Abubakar, A., & Murwa, A. (2018). Influence of planning of physical facilities on the provision of quality education in secondary schools in Kenya. *International Journal of Innovative Research and Development, 7*(5), 1-12. Retrieved from International Journal of Innovative Research and Development.
2. Adams, P. (2020). Blended learning models in higher education. *Journal of Digital Education.*
3. Altbach, P. G., Reisberg, L., & Rumbley, L. (2006). *Trends in global higher education: Tracking an academic revolution.* UNESCO 2009 World Conference on Higher Education.
4. Bloom, D., Canning, D., & Chan, K. (2006). Higher education and economic development in Africa. Harvard University; Human Development Sector, Africa Region.

5. Bloomfield Hills Schools. (n.d.). *Home.* Retrieved on 7/11/24 from https://www.bloomfield.org/
6. Bloom, D. E., Canning, D., & Chan, K. (2006). Higher education and economic development in Africa. *The World Bank.* Retrieved from https://openknowledge.worldbank.org/handle/10986/7990
7. Deslauriers, L., McCarty, L., Miller, K., Callaghan, K., & Kestin, G. (2019). Measuring actual learning versus feeling of learning in response to being actively engaged in the classroom. *Proceedings of the National Academy of Sciences, 116*(39), 19162–19167. https://doi.org/10.1073/pnas.1911069116
8. Government of Kenya. (2007). *Kenya Vision 2030: A globally competitive and prosperous Kenya.* Nairobi: Government Printer.
9. Juma, A. (2018). The influence of accommodation on the academic performance of university students. *International Journal of Current Research, 12*(4), 10900-10907. Retrieved from http://journalcra.com/article/influence-accommodation-academic-performance-university-students.
10. Kamau, E. (2015). Housing the next generation of Kenya's leaders: A PPP that makes the grade https://blogs.worldbank.org.
11. Kibera, A. (2017). The impact of inadequate facilities on students' academic life in higher education institutions in Kenya. *International Journal of Innovative Research & Development, 6*(7), 123-130. Retrieved from https://internationaljournalcorner.com/index.php/ijird_ojs/article/download/165254/113607/400415
12. Leong, W., & Hamzah, H. (2019). Harnessing public-private partnerships in the expansion of higher education facilities in Malaysia. *Journal of Higher Education Policy, 32*(1), 12-25.
13. Makokha, J. (2020). Address challenges faced by students residing off-campus. *Daily Nation.* Retrieved from https://nation.africa/kenya/news/address-challenges-faced-by-students-residing-off-campus--3586584
14. Makhanu, E. M., Nyongesa, W. M., & Wekesa, B. N. (2023). Effect of utilization of digital teaching materials on performance of learners in literature in public universities in Western Kenya. *Iconic Research And Engineering Journals, 7*(4), 526-535.

15. Mokaya, S. (2019). To what extent extracurricular activities affect the behaviors and academic performance of pupils. *International Journal of Education and Research, 7*(5), 1-12. Retrieved from SCIRP.
16. Ndirangu, M., & Udoto, M. O. (2011). Quality of learning facilities and learning environment: Challenges for teaching and learning in Kenya's public universities. *Quality Assurance in Education, 19*(3), 208-223. https://doi.org/10.1108/09684881311325829
17. Njoroge, M. (2018). The state of physical infrastructure in Kenyan universities: A challenge to quality education. *Education Infrastructure Review, 10*(2), 123-134.
18. Njuguna, C. W. (2019). Assessment of maintenance practices in public secondary schools in Kenya. *University of Nairobi.* Retrieved from University of Nairobi E-repository.
19. Nyabera, J. (2021). Exercise behavior and recreational sports participation predicts academic success. *University of the Pacific.* Retrieved from University of the Pacific Scholarly Common.
20. Nyerere, J. (2020). E-learning in Kenyan universities during COVID-19. *Journal of African Education, 25*(3), 45-60.
21. Odeo, I. I. (2020). Challenges facing new Kenyan higher education institutions: The case of Kibabii University. *Journal of Education and Practice, 11*(10), 1-10. Retrieved from [URL if available].
22. Odhiambo, B. M., & Khaemba, W. (2021). Influence of physical facilities on academic performance of students in public secondary schools in Kenya. *International Journal of Innovative Research and Development, 10*(3), 1-12. Retrieved from *International Journal of Innovative Research and Development.*
23. Okwach, T. O. (2018). Influence of ISO 9001:2008 quality management systems on academic staff service delivery in management of examinations in Kenya: A case study of public universities. *International Journal of Current Research, 10*(5), 69631–69644.
24. Oketch, M. (2003). The role of higher education in the socio-economic development of Kenya. *African Journal of Higher Education, 2*(2), 58-68.
25. Oketch, M. (2016). The challenges facing higher education in Kenya: A review of infrastructural inadequacies. *International Journal of Educational Studies, 9*(1), 10-22.
26. Onyango, J. O. (2020). Assessment of the maintenance culture of physical facilities in public universities in Kenya. *International Journal of*

Innovative Research and Development, 9(3), 1-12. Retrieved from *International Journal of Innovative Research and Development.*

27. Otieno, S. N. (2019). Challenges of student accommodation in public universities in Kenya: A case study of universities in Nairobi. *Journal of Higher Education, 28*(2), 145–160.
28. Sifuna, D. N. (2014). Challenges of funding in Kenyan higher education. *Kenya Educational Review.*
29. Teferra, D., & Altbach, P. G. (2004). African higher education: Challenges for the 21st century. *Higher Education: The International Journal of Higher Education and Educational Planning, 47*(1), 21-50.
30. UNESCO. (2017). *The impact of physical infrastructure on quality education.* UNESCO Institute for Statistics. Retrieved from https://uis.unesco.org/
31. Wekesa, N. J., & Kihoro, J. M. (2015). Challenges faced by university libraries in Kenya: A case study of public universities. *Journal of Information Science, 30*(3), 167-174.
32. World Bank. (2010). *Higher education in Africa: Challenges and opportunities.* World Bank Group. Retrieved from https://www.worldbank.org/
33. World Bank. (2017). *The World Bank Annual Report 2017.* Washington, DC: World Bank. https://hl.handle.net/10986/27986.

Chapter 4

Physical Facilities and Quality Learning Environment in Public Secondary Schools in Kenya

Kenya spends a substantial part of its budget on education, driven by the belief that education and training provide the greatest opportunity for equitable development and poverty reduction (Nielson, 2024). One objective of Kenya's educational system is to provide inclusive quality education to all learners, regardless of their socio-economic backgrounds, which is considered essential to promoting economic growth and expanding employment opportunities. However, some of the biggest challenges to achieving this, according to a government report on "Delivering Quality Education and Training to all Kenyans," include the provision of adequate and quality educational facilities in the face of increasing demand, and improving the quality of education provided (Republic of Kenya, 2005). The report further highlights that the demand for secondary school education far exceeds available places, particularly in urban slums where 60% of those needing secondary school education reside. This challenge is worsened by the slow expansion of secondary school infrastructure and an unfriendly learning environment.

Educational physical facilities encompass buildings, grounds, equipment, resource centers, and all other infrastructure provided to support the achievement of schools' learning objectives (Nduta, Itegi, Peter & Muchanje, 2024). The effectiveness of learning provided by a school is directly related to the quality and adequacy of its facilities. These facilities play an important role not only in fostering higher learner achievement but also in influencing other crucial aspects that promote better learning outcomes, such as creating a conducive learning environment that nurtures learners' sense of self-respect and self-worth (Walwe, 2011). Studies have shown that learner performance is not solely determined by intellectual ability and socio-economic background; other factors, such as self-concept and the learning environment, play an essential role (Bayer, 2000).

Not all learning spaces are equally effective in helping learners reach their full potential. Providing an inspirational learning environment that is safe and conducive for academic pursuits, and overall success is critical. Rawal Schools

(2024) note that an inspirational school must have basic facilities to meet the needs of students, teachers, and staff. These include adequate, well-equipped classrooms, a library with necessary reading materials, well-equipped science labs, and sports and sanitation facilities. Additional resources such as computer labs, cafeterias, and medical facilities also contribute to a quality learning environment, supporting learning, promoting students' health and safety, encouraging physical fitness, fostering innovation, and enhancing interaction within the school community.

Inadequate or inappropriate physical facilities hinder learners' ability to achieve their best academically. A study investigating the influence of school infrastructure on secondary school students' academic achievement concluded that there was a significant relationship between the availability of physical facilities and student motivation and academic success (Akomolafe & Adesua, 2016).

A common characteristic of Kenyan secondary schools is the overcrowding and overstretching of educational facilities (Shatuma, 2022). The Auditor General's report attributes this issue to underfunding in the Ministry of Education, poor needs assessment, under-budgeting, and a lack of guiding policy on infrastructural standards for schools. Additionally, there are no long-term plans for infrastructure development or improvement, resulting in inadequate and poorly maintained school facilities (Republic of Kenya, 2020).

The Ministry of Education's National Education Sector Strategic Plan for 2018–2022 indicates that 50% of secondary school-aged children are out of school and aims to achieve 100% transition from primary to secondary school. However, this goal is hindered by a lack of funds to create facilities that can accommodate the increasing number of students. Abuya, Maina, and Ogola's (2020) study on the status of secondary school education in Kenya, investigated several indicators of quality education, including academic achievement, infrastructure, and learning conditions. The study found that 68% of candidates who sat for the Kenya Certificate of Secondary Education failed by scoring an E grade, highlighting inefficiencies within the education system.

Overcrowded classrooms present serious challenges to the quality of education globally (Mankgele, 2023). In Kenya, class sizes in secondary schools generally range from 40 to 59 students. However, in counties like Turkana, Mandera, and

Garissa, teacher-to-student ratios can reach as high as 1 to 92, 1 to 80, and 1 to 67, respectively (Mutisya, 2020; Ndethiu, Masingila, Miheso-O'Connor, Khatete & Heath, 2017). Overcrowding hampers the teacher's ability to meet individual learners' needs, compromises the quality of learning, and often results in poor academic performance. Additionally, it deteriorates the learning environment through increased noise and disruptive behavior, indiscipline and presents health and safety risks by increasing disease transmission among students. Additionally, it impedes evacuation in case of emergencies such as school fires.

Quality of Physical Facilities and Learning Environment

The physical environment where learning occurs has a significant impact on students' behavior and academic performance (Schmidt, 2024). Since most of students' time in school is spent in the classrooms, this space is crucial for developing critical thinking skills and discovering talents. Well-organized classrooms provide an appropriate environment for learning efficiency (OZ Assignments, 2024).

Kenyan secondary school classrooms are generally arranged in rows facing the blackboard/whiteboard, which, while useful for orderliness, may hinder interaction and collaboration among learners (Hudson, 2024). Ideal classrooms promote student engagement by being well-lit, having good indoor air quality, and featuring visually appealing elements like painted walls and suitable furniture. They also allow for student-centred teaching approaches and enable teachers to employ a range of instructional techniques while maintaining discipline (OZ Assignments, 2024).

In a study on the influence of physical facilities on secondary education quality in Migori County, respondents rated the quality of classrooms and furniture as very low or low by 64.8% and 77%, respectively. Factors contributing to this include high enrollment rates and the semi-permanent nature of some structures. Inadequate and poorly constructed educational infrastructure in marginalized areas such as Turkana, Samburu, and North Eastern Kenya, further limit quality education. According to recent reports, over 250,000 children in Turkana are out of school due to insufficient classrooms and unsafe school buildings. Addressing these challenges requires targeted investment and innovative solutions like mobile schools and community-based learning. Collaboration between government, development partners, and local communities is crucial to sustainably improve educational infrastructure and, ultimately, the quality of education in these regions (UNESCO, 2006).

A study in Hamisi Sub-county, Kakamega County, found that the quality of classrooms and their physical conditions, such as ventilation, painting, and ceiling coverage, directly affected academic performance (Ndori, 2021). Unpainted walls, unventilated classrooms, and lack of ceilings contribute to unappealing learning spaces, impacting students' mood and motivation negatively. Clean, vibrant, and visually appealing environments help students feel pride and belonging in their schools (David J Smith Decorator Ltd., undated). However, given limited resources, schools often deprioritize aesthetic improvements like painting.

Library Facilities and Secondary Schools in Kenya

The school library plays a crucial role in fostering a culture of reading among students. The presence of a school library positively impacts student academic achievement and literacy by providing physical and digital spaces that host resources supporting students' and teachers' intellectual pursuits (Ouma & Nakitare, 2018). Field-Marsham (2023) observes that many secondary schools in Kenya lack libraries, noting that the absence of libraries in African countries poses a significant setback to achieving the United Nations Sustainable Development Goals (SDGs) on quality education. This is because it deprives students of access to necessary information, research tools, and problem-solving skills, which are vital for advancing their education and developing a passion for lifelong learning.

Mutungi, Minishi-Majanja, and Mnkeni-Saurombe (2014) observe that, despite the library being an essential resource in secondary schools, the Ministry of Education does not require a library as a prerequisite for a school's registration. In a study investigating the information literacy standards of school libraries in Nairobi and Tharaka-Nithi counties in Kenya, it was found that most schools lacked adequate libraries. The few existing libraries did not have up-to-date reading materials that would motivate student learning (Ireri, Evans & Ocholla, 2022). The poor academic performance in national examinations can, in part, be attributed to the absence of well-developed libraries and other information literacy resources.

Play Facilities in Secondary Schools in Kenya

Play facilities are essential in secondary schools as they support students' physical health, social skills, and overall well-being, enhancing their academic performance. However, many secondary schools in Kenya lack adequate play facilities, with available spaces often being overcrowded and under-resourced. According to Chege and Waithaka (2021), schools with quality play areas, such as well-maintained sports fields, courts, and recreational areas, provide students with opportunities for physical activities that relieve stress and promote teamwork.

The absence of sufficient play facilities is especially pronounced in densely populated urban schools, where limited land constrains the development of such amenities (Republic of Kenya, 2020). Studies show that without access to proper play areas, students may become disengaged, affecting their academic motivation and social behavior (Karanja & Gikandi, 2019). Additionally, overcrowded or poorly maintained play spaces can lead to safety concerns, increasing the risk of injury during physical activities (Mwangi, 2018).

Addressing this gap requires prioritizing play facilities as part of the school infrastructure investment, particularly in urban and resource-poor regions. Expanding access to safe and well-equipped play areas can create a balanced school environment that fosters physical, social, and cognitive growth (UNESCO, 2019).

Conclusion

In conclusion, the provision of adequate educational facilities is critical to the success of Kenya's educational system. While the country has made significant strides in funding education, the challenges of overcrowding, inadequate infrastructure, and insufficient resources persist, particularly in urban slums and marginalized areas. The lack of proper facilities—such as well-maintained classrooms, libraries, science labs, and play areas—directly impacts students' academic performance and well-being. Overcrowded classrooms, in particular, limit the effectiveness of teaching, disrupt student concentration, and heighten health risks. Similarly, insufficient or poorly equipped libraries hinder students' intellectual growth and limit their ability to develop crucial research and problem-solving skills.

Addressing these challenges requires a range of approaches, including increased investment in infrastructure, especially in high-demand areas, and the implementation of long-term maintenance plans. It is essential to prioritize the development of safe, functional, and inspiring learning environments that foster student engagement, motivation, and academic success. Collaborative efforts among the government, development partners, and local communities are necessary to achieve the goal of inclusive, quality education for all learners. Ultimately, improving school facilities will not only enhance academic outcomes but also contribute to the broader goal of poverty reduction and sustainable development, as education remains a key driver of economic and social progress.

References

1. Abuya, A. B., Maina, L., & Ogola, M. (2020). Study on the status of secondary education in Kenya. *Regional Education Learning Initiative*. Retrieved from https://rsisinternational.org/journals/ijriss/articles/sustainable-development-goal-for-education-the-case-of-kenyas-efforts-towards-universal-basic-education/
2. Akomolafe, M. J., & Adesua, A. (2016). Influence of school infrastructure on secondary school students' academic achievement. *Journal of Education and Practice, 7*(20), 46-50.
3. Bayer, L. (2000). Factors influencing learner performance: Intellectual ability, socio-economic background, and the learning environment.
4. Chege, F., & Waithaka, E. (2021). Pre-primary and lower primary teachers' professional identity in primary schools in Nairobi County, Kenya. *East African Journal of Education Studies, 3*(1), 223-232. https://doi.org/10.37284/eajes.3.1.391
5. David J. Smith Decorator Ltd. (n.d.). Importance of painting school buildings for learning environments. Retrieved from https://www.davidsmithdecorator.co.uk
6. Field-Marsham, R. C. (2023, April 23). School libraries key to achieving Sustainable Development Goals. Retrieved from https://keylibraries.org/

7. Hudson, T. (2024). Classroom seating – what's the best arrangement? *The Headteacher*. Retrieved from https://www.theheadteacher.com/attainment-and-assessment/teaching-practice/classroom-seating-whats-the-best-arrangement
8. Ireri, A., Evans, T., & Ocholla, D. (2022). Information literacy standards of school libraries in Nairobi and Tharaka-Nithi counties, Kenya. *Library Review, 71*(7), 1123-1136.
9. Karanja, J., & Gikandi, J. (2019). Influence of play facilities on children's academic motivation and social behavior in selected public primary schools in Nakuru County, Kenya. *European Scientific Journal, 15*(19), 8-19. https://doi.org/10.19044/esj.2019.v15n19p8
10. Mankgele, T. (2023). Teaching experiences with overcrowded classrooms in primary schools in the OR Tambo Coastal District of South Africa. *Asian Journal of Management, Entrepreneurship and Social Science, 3*(04), 1533-1545. Retrieved from https://ajmesc.com/index.php/ajmesc/article/view/620
11. Ministry of Education, Republic of Kenya. (2005). *Delivering quality education and training to all Kenyans*. Government Printer.
12. Mutisya, M. (2020). Managing overcrowded classrooms to accommodate learner-centered methodologies: An indispensable pillar for teachers' preparedness in implementation of competency-based curriculum in Kenya. *International Journal of Innovative Research & Development, 10*(11), 67-78. https://doi.org/10.24940/ijird/2021/v10/i11/NOV21002
13. Mutungi, B., Minishi-Majanja, M., & Mnkeni-Saurombe, N. (2016). The status of school libraries in Kenya: The case of public secondary schools in Nairobi County. *Mousaion: South African Journal of Information Studies, 32*(2), 150-172. https://doi.org/10.25159/0027-2639/1694
14. Mwangi, J. (2018). Influence of school playground safety on pre-school children's physical activity in Nairobi County, Kenya. [PDF document]. Retrieved from https://repository.anu.ac.ke/bitstream/
15. Ndethiu, M., Masingila, J., Miheso-O'Connor, P., Khatete, A., & Heath, M. (2017). Influence of school physical facilities on students' discipline in public secondary schools in Makueni County, Kenya. *International Journal of Innovative Research & Development, 5*(5), 258-263.
16. Ndori, M. D. (2021). Teachers' challenge of physical facilities on curriculum implementation in public day secondary schools in Hamisi Sub-

County, Kenya. *International Journal of Research and Innovation in Social Science, 5*(2), 419-426.

17. Nduta, B. G., Itegi, F. M., & Muchanje, P. N. (2024). Educational physical facilities and their influence on student achievement. *International Journal of Educational Research, 54*, 67-81.
18. Nielsen, H. (2024, January 27). An overview of the education system in Kenya. *Education Articles.*
19. Ouma, R., & Nakitare, G. (2018). Providing physical and digital spaces hosting resources that support student and teachers' intellectual pursuits. *Journal of Educational Technology, 10*(3), 34-42.
20. OZ Assignments. (2024). An ideal quality classroom: Facilitating student engagement and promoting positive learning environments. Retrieved from [URL]
21. Rawal Schools. (2024). An inspirational school must have basic facilities. Retrieved from https://www.rawalinternationalschool.com/
22. Republic of Kenya. (2005). *Delivering quality education and training to all Kenyans: Provision of adequate and quality educational facilities in the face of increasing demand, and improving the quality of education provided.*
23. Republic of Kenya. (2020). *National pre-primary education policy standard guidelines.* Retrieved from https://planipolis.iiep.unesco.org/sites/default/files/ressources/pre-primary_policy_guidelines_11_1.pdf
24. Republic of Kenya. (2020). *Auditor General Report.* Government Printer.
25. Schmidt, R. J. (2024). The impact of the physical environment on K-12 students. Retrieved from https://www.linkedin.com/pulse/impact-physical-environment-k-12-students-dr-raymond-j-schmidt-auutf
26. Shatuma, J. (2022). A general characteristic in the Kenyan secondary school scene is educational facilities that are overstretched and overcrowded. Retrieved from https://www.the-star.co.ke/news/2022-02-05/public-schools-lack-long-term-infrastructure-plans--report
27. UNESCO. (2006). *Global education digest 2006: Comparing education statistics across the world.* UNESCO Institute for Statistics. Retrieved from https://uis.unesco.org/sites/default/files/documents/global-education-digest-2006-comparing-education-statistics-across-the-world-en_0.pdf

28. UNESCO. (2019). *School infrastructure: A key to quality education.* Retrieved from https://policytoolbox.iiep.unesco.org/policy-option/school-infrastructure/
29. Walwe, J. (2011). The relationship between perception of the state of school physical facilities and classroom learning environment on students' self-concept in secondary schools in Taita-Taveta District, Kenya. Unpublished M.Ed thesis, Egerton University.

Chapter 5

Influence Adequacy of Physical Facilities and Quality of TVET in Kenya

Technical Vocational Education and Training (TVET) represents a critical component in the educational landscape, particularly in developing countries like Kenya. Defined as the educational processes that encompass general education, technology studies, and the acquisition of practical skills, TVET aims at equipping individuals with the competencies required for various occupations (UNESCO, 2020). The significance of TVET lies not only in its ability to provide vocational skills but also in its potential to drive economic growth and industrial development. As noted by Abdallah and Zafar (2018), countries that invest in TVET can create a skilled workforce, crucial for economic transformation.

A well-trained workforce is crucial for enhancing labour productivity, reducing unemployment, and improving living standards. According to Kanayo (2013), nations with inadequate skill levels often experience slow economic growth. The differences in social and economic development among countries frequently reflect the varying skill levels of their labour forces, which directly impacts productivity. This relationship underlines the importance of effective Technical and Vocational Education and Training programs designed to bridge the skills gap and promote economic resilience. TVET equips individuals with practical skills tailored to meet the demands of the labour market, thereby addressing the skills mismatch that many employers face (World of TVET, n.d.). Countries that prioritize TVET often see significant reductions in unemployment rates, as these programs create a direct pathway to stable employment (World Bank et al., 2023). Furthermore, investing in quality TVET not only enhances individual livelihoods but also stimulates broader economic growth by fostering a more skilled workforce capable of adapting to changing industry needs (Asadullah, 2019). Ultimately, strengthening TVET systems is essential for achieving sustainable economic development and social equity

Global Perspectives on TVET

Many countries in the world have recognized the benefits of TVET. In the United States, TVET programs align closely with career pathways in fields such as agriculture, architecture, and finance (UNESCO-UNEVOC, 2014). This alignment ensures that educational outcomes meet labour market demands, providing students with viable employment options upon graduation. Germany exemplifies a successful model where 80% of vocational education occurs in industry, emphasizing a dual system that combines classroom learning with practical, employer-driven training (UNDP, 2012; Deissinger, 2015). This model's effectiveness is evidenced by the fact that two-thirds of young people aged 22 years pursue apprenticeship training, with a 75% completion rate, facilitating their transition into the workforce (Abdukarim & Ali, 2012).

India's National Skill Development Corporation (NSDC) collaborates with private sector companies to design and deliver industry-relevant training programs. Through the Skill India initiative, the NSDC aims to train over 400 million people in various trades by 2025. For instance, partnerships with industries such as automotive and telecommunications ensure that training programs remain up-to-date with industry standards, making graduates more employable. According to Maitra, Maitra, and Thakur (2022), this initiative has led to improved job placement rates and a workforce better equipped to support India's growing economy. This is an example of a proactive engagement that helps to align educational outcomes with industry requirements, ultimately enhancing trainees' employability.

In Africa, TVET is viewed as a vital aspect for national development. Dasmani (2011) notes that interest in TVET grew in the 1970s, driven by the need to address skilled labour shortages in newly independent countries. Nations such as Zimbabwe, South Africa, and Ghana have made substantial investments in TVET, viewing it as a pathway to prepare citizens for a dynamic work environment. However, the effectiveness of these programs is often hampered by limited industry involvement in curriculum development and funding, leading to a disconnect between the training provided and market demands (Kigwilu, 2016).

TVET in Kenya: Policy Framework and Challenges

In Kenya, TVET is positioned as a key driver for achieving the Vision 2030 agenda, which aims at transforming the country into a newly industrialized middle-income economy with a high standard of living by the year 2030 (Republic of Kenya, 2012). This ambitious goal necessitates a workforce equipped with relevant skills capable of producing competitive industrial products and services. Youth Polytechnics, as integral part of the TVET system, are expected to provide quality training that aligns with market demands.

Despite the policy framework, reports indicate that many TVET graduates possess a lot of theoretical knowledge but lack practical and interpersonal and critical thinking skills necessary for success at the workplace (UNDP, 2012). Studies conducted by Agufana and Ndaviula (2011) and Kamau (2013) highlight significant deficiencies in infrastructure and equipment, as well as instructional resources, undermining the quality of education provided. The status of physical facilities in Technical and Vocational Education and Training (TVET) institutions in Kenya varies widely depending on the region, institutional size, and funding availability.

The Role of Physical Facilities in TVET

Physical facilities in educational contexts refer to the various infrastructures that support both academic and non-academic activities. These include classrooms, workshops, libraries, laboratories, and recreational spaces. Adequate physical facilities play a crucial role in the instructional process by enhancing the learning environment and facilitating effective teaching methods. According to Biyabeyen (2014), well-equipped facilities enable educators to demonstrate concepts clearly, provide hands-on experiences, and employ instructional strategies that promote critical thinking and engagement. Conversely, inadequate facilities can lead to disengagement among learners and hinder their academic performance.

State of Physical Facilities in TVET Institutions

The current state of physical facilities in TVET institutions in Kenya is of great concern. Kings (2005) reported that many educational facilities are insufficient and in a state of disrepair, creating barriers to effective teaching and learning. A study conducted in Kisii County showed that youth polytechnics suffered from a lack of essential resources such as classrooms, workshops, and libraries, which are critical for delivering quality education. In many cases, available facilities were old, dilapidated, and dysfunctional, limiting the ability of educators to engage students effectively (Obare, Wamutitu, Ndirangu, 2021.) For example, many rural youth polytechnics are under-resourced resulting in poorly equipped workshops or lack of modern tools. Institutions like those in West Pokot, and Kisii Counties struggle with outdated or insufficient equipment, limiting acquisition of practical skills (Luyali, Olel & Othuon, 2015).

Inadequate infrastructure negatively impacts the learning experience. Dilapidated buildings and obsolete teaching equipment can frustrate both learners and educators (Duruji et al., 2014). Many youth polytechnics were established in the 1970s and 1980s, often with the support of non-governmental organizations. However, a lack of ongoing funding has left them struggling to maintain or upgrade their facilities (Sigei & Ngahu 2023). Additionally, Muendo (2016) highlighted issues of overcrowding due to insufficient furniture and other resources, leading to compromised learning environments.

Importance of Workshops and Learning Resources

In vocational fields such as mechanical engineering and electrical installation, the adequacy of workshops and tools is critical for skill acquisition. Obare, et al; (2021) found that many youth polytechnics in Kisii County were poorly equipped, contradicting government regulations that require adequate workshops and laboratories for TVET institutions (ROK, 2015). The absence of well-equipped facilities limits practical training opportunities, resulting in inadequate preparation for the job market. Studies further showed that an improvement in availability of physical facilities such as workshops, ICT infrastructure and classrooms, improved on student enrolment, retention and achievement (Mwangi, 2015). The lack of ICT facilities in youth polytechnics limits student engagement and hinders effective learning. Traditional teaching methods prevail, restricting hands-on and interactive learning essential for developing technical skills. Integrating technology fosters student motivation, global connectivity, and practical experience, improving both learning outcomes and economic resilience (Bhat, 2023; Mdpi, 2022)

Library Facilities and Quality Education

deficiencies in library resources, echoing findings by Ngware (2002) and Nasongo et al. (2013), which highlighted the absence of basic teaching materials in many institutions. A well-stocked library is essential for enhancing academic achievement and supporting effective content delivery; conversely, inadequate resources can lead to ineffective instructional methods that hinder skill acquisition.

The absence of sufficient library facilities restricts access to vital reference materials for both students and instructors, affecting the depth of knowledge students can acquire and diminishing the overall quality of education. A study conducted in Nyeri County found that 51.6% of TVET institutions lacked libraries altogether, severely undermining their ability to provide comprehensive educational experiences (Kigwilu & Akala, 2017). Furthermore, the lack of modern ICT facilities exacerbates this issue, as over 80% of TVET institutions reported inadequate access to necessary technology that supports learning and research (Obare et al., 2021).

Consequences for Skill Acquisition

These deficiencies in library facilities correlate directly with poor academic performance and limited skill acquisition among students. Walking (2001) emphasized that practical sessions following theoretical instruction are essential for effective learning; however, without adequate resources like libraries and workshops, institutions struggle to provide these opportunities. The lack of exposure to diverse learning materials hampers students' ability to engage critically with their subjects, ultimately affecting their job market readiness. Improving library facilities within TVET institutions is crucial for enhancing educational quality and ensuring that students acquire the necessary skills for their future careers. Addressing these infrastructural gaps will require targeted interventions from policymakers and educational authorities to allocate resources effectively and promote a conducive learning environment.

Challenges Facing TVET Institutions

The challenges facing TVET institutions in Kenya are complex and well-established. Inadequate infrastructure, poor funding, and limited industry involvement in curriculum development contribute to the systemic issues plaguing the TVET sector. The reliance on government funding alone hampers the ability of institutions to maintain and upgrade their facilities, resulting in outdated resources that fail to meet current industry standards.

Furthermore, the lack of collaboration between TVET institutions and the private sector creates a disconnect between training programs and market needs. Employers often express concerns about the preparedness of graduates, citing gaps in practical skills and industry-relevant knowledge (Kamau, 2013). This misalignment underscores the need for a comprehensive approach that integrates industry input into the design and implementation of TVET programs.

Recommendations for Improvement

To enhance the quality of TVET in Kenya, several recommendations can be made:

1. **Increased Government Investment**: The government should allocate more funds to improve the physical infrastructure of TVET institutions, ensuring that facilities meet modern educational standards.
2. **Industry Collaboration**: Strengthening partnerships between TVET institutions and industry stakeholders can ensure that training programs are aligned with market demands. Involving employers in curriculum development can enhance the relevance of educational offerings.
3. **Community Engagement**: Engaging local communities in the management and maintenance of TVET facilities can foster a sense of ownership and accountability, leading to better upkeep of resources.
4. **Sustainable Practices**: Adopting sustainable building practices and technologies can enhance the quality and longevity of educational infrastructure while promoting environmental responsibility.
5. **Continuous Professional Development**: Investing in the professional development of educators can ensure they are equipped with the latest teaching methodologies and industry knowledge, improving the overall quality of instruction.

6. **Monitoring and Evaluation**: A rigorous monitoring and evaluation tracking system would be necessary to ensure effectiveness of TVET programs and infrastructure investments, ensuring accountability and continuous improvement.

Conclusion

Adequacy of physical facilities plays a crucial role in enhancing the quality of TVET in Kenya. The current state of these facilities, particularly in rural youth polytechnics, reveals significant gaps that hinder effective teaching and learning. Limited resources, outdated equipment, and overcrowded classrooms have compromised the quality of education, resulting in graduates who are ill-prepared for the workforce. To address these shortcomings, it is imperative for the Kenyan government to increase investment in infrastructure, modernize workshops, and strengthen ICT capabilities. Additionally, fostering closer collaboration between TVET institutions and industry stakeholders is essential to ensure that training programs are relevant and aligned with market needs. By engaging communities in facility maintenance and focusing on continuous professional development for educators, Kenya can create a robust TVET system that supports economic growth and provides skilled individuals capable of meeting industry demands. Strategic reforms, monitoring, and evaluation are necessary for achieving these goals and improving TVET outcomes.

References

1. Abdallah, R., & Zafar, M. (2018). *Skills development for economic transformation in developing countries*. Nairobi: Kenya Institute for Public Policy Research and Analysis.
2. Abdulkarim, I., & Ali, M. (2012). Vocational education and poverty reduction: A tool for sustainable development in Nigeria. *Journal of Developing Countries Studies, 2*(2), 67–73. https://doi.org/10.1.1.861.2236
3. Asadullah, M. N. (2019). The impact of vocational education on income growth and employment. *Journal of Vocational Education & Training, 71*(2), 251–271.

4. Agufana, A., & Ndaviula, R. (2011). *Assessing the challenges facing TVET in Kenya.* Nairobi: University of Nairobi Press.
5. Biyabeyen, A. (2014). Impact of physical facilities on quality education in secondary schools in Kenya. *Journal of Educational Research.*
6. Bhat, R. A. (2023). The impact of technology integration on student learning outcomes: A comparative study. *International Journal of Social Science, Educational, Economics, Agriculture Research, and Technology (IJSET), 2*(9), 593–594.
7. Dasmani, I. (2011). The role of technical and vocational education and training in African development. *African Journal of Economic Policy.*
8. Deissinger, T. (2015). The dual system of vocational education and training in Germany: A model for other countries? *Journal of Vocational Education & Training.*
9. Duruji, M. M., et al. (2014). Challenges of vocational education and training in Nigeria: A review. *International Journal of Vocational Education and Training Research.*
10. Kamau, S. M. (2013). Challenges affecting the technical and vocational education training youth polytechnics in Kiambu County. *International Journal of Social Sciences and Entrepreneurship, 1*(5), 679–687.
11. Kanayo, K. O. (2013). The impact of human capital formation on economic growth in Nigeria. *Journal of Economics, 4*(2), 121–132. https://doi.org/10.1080/09765239.2013.11884972
12. Kigwilu, P. C., & Akala, W. J. (2017). Resource utilization and curriculum implementation in community colleges in Kenya: Towards inclusive education. *IOSR Journal of Research & Method in Education, 7*(3), 21–29. https://doi.org/10.9790/7388-0703012129
13. Kings, L. (2005). The impact of infrastructure on educational outcomes in Kenya. *Journal of Educational Administration.*
14. Luyali, E. P., Olel, A. M., & Othuon, L. (2015). Enrolment trends in youth polytechnics in West Pokot County, Kenya. https://repository.maseno.ac.ke/handle/123456789/1640 Maitra, S., Maitra, S., & Thakur, M. (2022). Uncertain itineraries: Dual system of training and contemporary TVET reforms in India. *Journal of Vocational Education and Training.* https://doi.org/10.1080/13636820.2022.2042724 (Early Online Publication)
15. MDPI. (2022). The role of ICT in improving education outcomes. *MDPI Education Journal.*

https://www.mdpi.com/education/technology-integration

16. Muendo, W. (2016). Challenges of resource availability in youth polytechnics in Kenya: A case study of Machakos County. *Journal of Education and Practice*.
17. Mwangi, F. M. (2015). Factors influencing implementation of projects in public secondary schools in Mathira Constituency, Nyeri County, Kenya: Unpublished research project, University of Nairobi.
18. Nasongo, J., et al. (2013). Quality in technical and vocational education and training: Perspectives from stakeholders in Kenya. *International Journal of Technical Education and Training*.
19. Ngware, M. W. (2002). Gender participation in technical training institutions: An assessment of the Kenyan case. *Eastern Africa Social Science Research Review, 18*(1), 21–33.
20. Obare, M. M., Wamutitu, J. M., & Ndirangu, M. (2020). Influence of adequacy of physical facilities on quality of youth polytechnic graduates in Kisii County. *Journal of Education & Pedagogy, 12*(2), 1–12.
21. Republic of Kenya. (2012). *Vision 2030: The popular version*. Nairobi: Government Printer.
22. Republic of Kenya. (2015). *TVET Act, 2013: An overview*. Nairobi: Government Printer.
23. Sigei, D. K., & Ngahu, S. (2023). Budgeting and performance of youth polytechnics in Nakuru County, Kenya. *Journal of Economics and Finance (IOSR-JEF), 14*(5), 28–34.
24. UNESCO. (2020). *Technical and vocational education and training in Africa: A policy brief*. Paris: UNESCO.
25. UNESCO-UNEVOC. (2014). *Global inventory of regional and national qualifications frameworks*. Bonn: UNESCO-UNEVOC.
26. UNDP. (2012). *Skills for inclusive growth in Kenya: A policy review*. Nairobi: United Nations Development Programme.
27. World Bank, International Labour Organization, & UNESCO. (2023). *Building better formal TVET systems: Principles and practice in low- and middle-income countries*. World Bank Publications.
28. World of TVET. (n.d.). Economic impact of vocational education: Skills, jobs, and prosperity. Retrieved from https://www.worldoftvet.com/blog/economic-impact-of-vocational-education

Chapter 6

Lessons from Kenya's Change to Competency-Based Curriculum

Countries often overhaul their curricula in response to evolving educational needs, global economic demands, and societal changes. One primary reason for this is the need to equip students with relevant skills that align with modern job markets, particularly in fields like science and technology, where rapid advancements necessitate updated content and pedagogical approaches (Dumont et al., 2010). Additionally, educational reforms may be driven by a desire to address disparities in student outcomes, ensuring that all learners have equitable access to quality education (OECD, 2012). Furthermore, curricula may be revised to incorporate values of critical thinking, creativity, and collaboration. Success in the 21st century is often argued to depend on the possession of these skills (Schleicher, 2018). Such comprehensive reforms aim not only to enhance academic achievement but also to foster holistic development, preparing students to navigate and contribute positively to a complex, interconnected world.

Kenya decided to overhaul its curriculum and adopt the Competency-Based Curriculum (CBC) in response to several key factors aimed at enhancing the quality of education. One significant motivation was the need to shift from a purely examination-oriented system to one that focuses on the development of critical thinking, creativity, and practical skills among learners (Ministry of Education, 2017). The previous 8-4-4 system was criticized for being rigid and not adequately preparing students for the demands of the modern workplace (Gikandi, 2019). Additionally, the CBC aims to address educational disparities by providing a more inclusive framework that caters to diverse learner needs and promotes holistic development (KNEC, 2020). This reform aligns with global trends emphasizing competency-based education, ensuring that Kenyan students acquire relevant skills necessary for success in a dynamic and competitive world (Kibera, 2019).

A Competency-Based Curriculum (CBC) is an educational framework that emphasizes the development of skills, knowledge, and attitudes required for learners to perform tasks effectively and meet specific standards in both academic and real-world contexts. Unlike traditional education systems that often focus on content mastery within a fixed timeframe, CBC emphasizes the learner's ability to demonstrate competency or mastery of skills, regardless of the time taken. This approach aims to equip students with the practical skills and problem-solving abilities necessary for success in both professional and personal environments (Gervais, 2016).

Core Principles of Competency-Based Curriculum

One of the key principles of CBC is learner-centeredness. This approach shifts the focus from a curriculum designed to meet the needs of all learners to one that emphasizes learning paths personalized to each learner's strengths, needs, and interests. By doing so, the CBC enhances motivation and engagement, allowing learners to advance through content as they demonstrate mastery of skills rather than progressing simply due to time spent in class. According to Spady (1994), a CBC framework promotes "learner empowerment" by giving students control over their learning journey, fostering greater responsibility and self-discipline.

Another critical aspect of CBC is the emphasis on relevance. The curriculum is designed to include competencies that align closely with real-life situations and professional requirements. This means that the skills acquired are directly applicable in the workforce, bridging the gap between educational institutions and labor market demands. As Dall'Alba and Sandberg (2006) argue that CBC enables students to "develop practical expertise," ensuring they are prepared for complex and dynamic environments.

Benefits of Competency-Based Curriculum

The CBC approach presents several benefits. Firstly, it promotes holistic development by incorporating cognitive, social, and emotional skills within the learning process. CBC frameworks are typically structured around specific competencies, such as critical thinking, communication, creativity, and collaboration, often referred to as "21st-century skills" (Trilling & Fadel, 2009). These competencies are increasingly being recognized as crucial for success in today's globalized and technology-driven world.

Secondly, CBC fosters continuous assessment rather than periodic examinations. Assessments in a CBC system are formative and ongoing, allowing educators to track students' progress in real-time and offer immediate feedback. This type of assessment enhances learning, as students receive continuous information on their strengths and areas needing improvement. Consequently, the pressure associated with high-stakes testing is reduced, promoting a more in-depth understanding of the material (Guskey, 2015). The Competency-Based Curriculum offers an innovative and flexible approach to education that prepares learners to meet the demands of the modern world. By prioritizing skills and attitudes alongside academic knowledge, CBC helps create well-rounded individuals equipped to handle complex challenges. However, its success largely depends on adequate resources, policy support, and stakeholder buy-in. As educational systems worldwide continue to evolve, CBC serves as a model on how education can be made more relevant and impactful.

Strategies for Effective CBC Curriculum Implementation

An approach that ensures the curriculum meets diverse learner needs and prepares them for real-world challenges should prioritize the following:

1. **Stakeholder Engagement**
   Involving all relevant stakeholders—government agencies, educators, parents, learners, and private sector partners—ensures buy-in and a shared understanding of the CBC's goals. Stakeholder engagement helps align resources, expectations, and support for implementation. Studies suggest that when stakeholders understand and support educational reforms, outcomes are significantly improved (Fullan, 2007). Partnerships with the private sector can also bring additional resources and expertise, which are crucial for creating a sustainable CBC model.

2. **Teacher Preparation and Continuous Professional Development**
   Teachers are the primary drivers of CBC implementation. Consequently, comprehensive training and ongoing professional development are essential. Educators need a clear understanding of competency-based assessment, differentiated instruction, and practical teaching methods. Research by Darling-Hammond et al. (2009) highlights that teachers who receive targeted professional development are more effective in student-centered learning environments, a cornerstone of CBC. Consequently, investing in teacher readiness can significantly impact CBC's success.

3. **Infrastructure and Resource Investment**
Effective CBC implementation also requires investment in infrastructure, including classrooms, technology, and learning materials, to facilitate competency development. In Kenya, for example, gaps in school facilities have hindered the successful implementation of new curricula (Wanjiru & Mugo, 2018). Equipping schools with adequate resources ensures students have hands-on learning experiences essential for competency-based education.

4. **Continuous Assessment and Feedback**
CBC relies heavily on formative assessments, where students receive ongoing feedback to track progress and development. This allows for timely interventions to address learning gaps. Marzano (2006) advocates for assessment systems that continuously inform students and educators, enabling adaptive teaching strategies and promoting continuous improvement in learning outcomes.

Competency-Based Curriculum: Successes and Challenges

A successful example of Competency-Based Curriculum implementation is evident in Finland's education system, which has consistently ranked among the top global performers in educational outcomes (Sahlberg, 2015). Finland's adoption of CBC emphasizes individualized learning paths, where students progress at their own pace while demonstrating competencies in skills like problem-solving, collaboration, and critical thinking. This approach is supported by a robust framework for teacher support, including continuous professional development, adequate resources, and a focus on teacher autonomy (Niemi & Isopahkala-Bouret, 2015). Finland's CBC success is attributed to its well-prepared teaching workforce, decentralized curriculum tailored to local needs, and a strong social commitment to equity in education. Additionally, Finland's low reliance on high-stakes testing allows students to focus on genuine understanding rather than memorization (Sahlberg, 2015).

Several African countries, including South Africa, Uganda, Rwanda, and Kenya, have also attempted to adopt the competency-based curriculum. In South Africa, initial optimism accompanied CBC's introduction in 1997, but it faced numerous challenges due to inadequate teacher training, large class sizes, and limited resources. Teachers reported that the curriculum was complex and challenging to implement, leading to the reform being abandoned, as noted in the 2012 Curriculum and Assessment Policy Statement (CAPS). CAPS retained competency-oriented aspects but simplified content and assessment procedures (Spaull, 2019).

In 2020, Uganda introduced CBC reforms in secondary school education, focusing on creating a skills-based, practical learning environment that prioritizes critical thinking, use of technology, and communication skills. However, implementation has been hindered by resource shortages and insufficient teacher training. A significant portion of Uganda's education budget is allocated to teacher salaries, leaving limited funds for resources and ongoing professional development (Muwagga & Kakooza, 2021). As a result, many teachers struggle to deliver CBC effectively, particularly in under-resourced rural areas. Additionally, Uganda's high student-to-teacher ratios present challenges for the individualized attention that CBC typically requires.

Rwanda has been the most successful among these nations. The country introduced a Competency-Based Curriculum in 2015, aiming to create a more learner-centered approach that emphasizes skills like critical thinking, creativity, and problem-solving (National Institute of Statistics Rwanda (NISR), 2018). Rwanda's CBC has shown early success in fostering practical skills and encouraging active classroom engagement. Teachers report that the curriculum has helped students become more confident and adaptable learners. However, challenges remain, particularly with resource availability and teacher preparation. Many teachers in Rwanda were initially unfamiliar with CBC methodologies, necessitating continuous training and support (Kabanza, 2019). Additionally, rural schools often struggle to provide the resources needed for CBC, resulting in disparities in learning outcomes across regions.

The implementation of Kenya's Competency-Based Curriculum (CBC) has encountered multiple challenges, from infrastructural inadequacies to training deficiencies and financial constraints. A critical issue is the lack of sufficient resources and facilities, as many schools face shortages in classrooms, learning materials, and equipment necessary for the hands-on, skills-based learning that CBC demands (Owino & Ndiku, 2021). Additionally, teachers have often been unprepared to transition from the content-focused 8-4-4 system to CBC, which emphasizes competency and practical skills. According to a study by Odongo and Okoth (2020), many teachers report inadequate training and support, impacting their confidence and effectiveness in delivering the curriculum. Financial limitations further hinder implementation, as both schools and parents struggle with the costs associated with CBC, including specialized learning materials and assessments. Waweru (2019) observes that limited government funding has forced schools to rely heavily on parents, creating disparities in access and exacerbating inequality among students from different socioeconomic backgrounds. These challenges point to the need for systemic support, increased funding, and continuous teacher training to ensure effective CBC implementation in Kenya.

Teacher readiness is the cornerstone of CBC's success, as this approach requires educators to shift from a traditional, exam-oriented model to one focused on individualized learning and continuous assessment. However, many Kenyan teachers report insufficient training, with many struggling to deliver competency-based instruction effectively. Teachers indicate they lack the necessary skills and support to implement CBC effectively, resulting in inconsistent delivery across schools (Mwangi & Chege, 2020). Rwanda recognized early on that teacher readiness is essential for successful CBC implementation. The Rwandan government invested in extensive teacher training programs to equip teachers with the skills needed for learner-centered instruction. Continuous professional development is also integrated to ensure that teachers are prepared to handle CBC challenges—an approach that could benefit Kenya, where teacher preparation has been a major challenge (Kabanza, 2019).

Implementing Kenya's CBC has proven costly, with expenses for new materials, teacher training, and infrastructure upgrades often passed on to parents, who must purchase additional learning materials. This financial burden has led to significant resistance from parents, particularly in lower-income communities, where affording these costs is challenging (Nyamwembe & Ombati, 2020).

At the same time, the transition from the 8-4-4 system, which emphasized exams and rote learning, to CBC has faced resistance from teachers, parents, and even students. Many stakeholders were not adequately informed about CBC's objectives and benefits, leading to misconceptions and resistance. This resistance often stems from a lack of familiarity with CBC principles and the perception that the new system is burdensome and complex (Waweru, 2019).

Successful CBC implementation requires clear, consistent policies and strong support from educational authorities. Rwanda's CBC model is dynamic, with continuous assessments and adaptations based on feedback from educators, students, and other stakeholders. For example, periodic reviews ensure that the curriculum remains relevant and aligns with labor market needs. Kenya could benefit from a similar feedback mechanism, allowing for flexible improvements and reducing resistance from teachers and parents. In Kenya, however, a lack of clear policy guidelines has caused confusion among educators and school administrators regarding expectations and assessment criteria. Additionally, coordination between the Ministry of Education and other relevant bodies has sometimes been lacking, which hinders a seamless rollout and monitoring of the curriculum (Odhiambo, 2021).

CBC ideally requires smaller class sizes to facilitate personalized learning and continuous assessment, as the curriculum emphasizes that students' progress at their own pace based on mastery rather than age or grade level. Smaller classes allow teachers to provide targeted support, monitor individual progress, and deliver the feedback essential for competency-based education. However, many Kenyan public schools are characterized by large class sizes, with student-teacher ratios often exceeding recommended levels. This has made it challenging for teachers to address individual student needs, undermining the personalized approach integral to CBC (Mwangi & Chege, 2020).

Research by Otieno and Njoroge (2021) indicates that overcrowded classrooms hinder teachers' ability to implement formative assessments, which are central to CBC's learning model. In such settings, students often miss out on the individualized attention necessary to develop critical skills and competencies. Similarly, Kimani (2019) observes that in schools with large class sizes, teachers often face time constraints, making it difficult to support students who need additional guidance or alternative instructional approaches. The Kenya Institute of Curriculum Development (KICD) (2022) has also acknowledged that large class sizes compromise CBC's effectiveness, as teachers cannot conduct the differentiated teaching and ongoing assessment required for each student's development. Consequently, the overcrowded conditions prevalent in many Kenyan schools not only undermine CBC's effectiveness but also perpetuate disparities in learning outcomes, particularly in underserved regions where teacher shortages exacerbate the issue (Ngugi & Wanjiru, 2020).

Rushed Rollout: The Risks and Consequences of Implementing Kenya's CBC

The rushed rollout of Kenya's CBC has deviated from the ideal phased approach that would typically allow for a smoother adaptation of curriculum changes across a complex and diverse educational landscape. In an ideal setting, a phased approach offers an opportunity to build institutional capacity, allocate resources effectively, and refine strategies based on pilot studies and feedback from stakeholders, thereby enhancing the curriculum's impact and sustainability (Odhiambo, 2021).

A gradual implementation would have provided time to train teachers comprehensively, a crucial process for shifting from the content-based 8-4-4 system to the skills-focused CBC. According to Wanjohi and Muthoni (2020), effective teacher training and preparation are foundational to CBC's success, yet in Kenya, many teachers were expected to implement the curriculum without adequate professional development. This lack of preparatory time has led to challenges in instructional delivery, as teachers are often ill-equipped to adopt CBC's learner-centered approaches. Moreover, a phased model could have provided time to address infrastructural deficiencies, particularly in under-resourced schools. Njoroge (2022) notes that CBC's resource demands—such as new textbooks, ICT facilities, and practical materials—require significant investment which a rushed approach fails to account for, leaving schools unable to fully meet these needs.

Furthermore, a gradual implementation allows for a feedback loop where stakeholders, including teachers, parents, and students, can provide input, enabling adjustments to be made based on real classroom experiences. This iterative refinement process is vital for curriculum effectiveness in any education system (Mutiso, 2021). Additionally, Sifuna (2019) emphasizes that a rushed implementation risks widening educational inequalities, as schools in low-income areas often lack the infrastructure, staff, and materials necessary to support a new curriculum without comprehensive support. Ultimately, a phased approach not only ensures resource alignment but also enables educational institutions to adapt to systemic changes in a way that supports equitable access and long-term success.

The implementation of Kenya's Competency-Based Curriculum (CBC) has had mixed results in achieving its objectives. While CBC was designed to address the limitations of the previous 8-4-4 system and promote skills development, critical thinking, and holistic learner development, various challenges have hindered its full realization. CBC implementation deviates from ideal curriculum practices primarily due to a lack of adequate preparation, insufficient teacher training, and inadequate stakeholder engagement. Addressing these deviations requires a more inclusive approach, sustained teacher support, robust investment in infrastructure, and a comprehensive monitoring and evaluation framework. This would enable a more effective implementation process that aligns with CBC's objectives and maximizes its impact on learners.

Conclusion

While Kenya's adoption of the Competency-Based Curriculum (CBC) presents a promising shift towards skills-focused education, its implementation has faced significant challenges. The lack of adequate teacher training, insufficient resources, and infrastructural deficits have hindered the full realization of CBC's potential. Resistance from parents and stakeholders, coupled with financial constraints, has further complicated the transition from the traditional 8-4-4 system. However, lessons can be drawn from successful implementations in countries like Finland and Rwanda, where comprehensive teacher preparation, ongoing professional development, and strong stakeholder engagement have been pivotal. For Kenya to achieve the intended outcomes of CBC, it must prioritize a phased implementation approach, invest in teacher readiness, and address the resource gaps that limit its effectiveness. With sustained commitment, strategic policy support, and proper resource allocation, Kenya can realize the CBC's vision of producing well-rounded, skilled individuals equipped with the competencies demanded by a dynamic global economy."

References

1. Dall'Alba, G., & Sandberg, J. (2006). Developing practical expertise: Teaching and learning in practice. *Education and Training, 48*(8), 602–612. https://doi.org/10.1108/00400910610717115
2. Darling-Hammond, L., Wei, R. C., Andree, A., Richardson, N., & Orphanos, S. (2009). Professional learning in the learning profession: A

status report on teacher development in the United States and abroad. National Staff Development Council.

3. Dumont, H., Istance, D., & Benavides, F. (2010). The nature of learning: Using research to inspire practice. OECD Publishing.
4. Fullan, M. (2007). *The new meaning of educational change*. Routledge.
5. Gathigia, M. G., & Nyambura, S. (2020). Resource challenges in the implementation of CBC in rural Kenyan schools. *Educational Review Journal, 72*(2), 140–155. https://doi.org/10.1080/00131911.2019.1696223
6. Gervais, J. (2016). The operational definition of competency-based education. *The Journal of Competency-Based Education, 1*(1), 1–10. https://doi.org/10.1002/cbe2.1023
7. Gikandi, J. W. (2019). *Challenges and opportunities of CBC in Kenyan education*. Nairobi University Press.
8. Guskey, T. R. (2015). *On your mark: Challenging the conventions of grading and reporting*. Solution Tree Press.
9. Kabanza, A. (2019). Challenges in implementing competency-based curriculum in Rwanda: Teacher preparedness and training needs. *Rwanda Education Board.*
10. Kenya Institute of Curriculum Development. (2022). *Competency-based curriculum implementation challenges: Large class sizes and teacher capacity*. Kenya Institute of Curriculum Development.
11. Kenya National Examinations Council. (2020). *Assessment strategies under the competency-based curriculum*. Kenya National Examinations Council.
12. Kibera, L. W. (2019). The relevance of competency-based curriculum in the Kenyan context. *Education and Development Studies, 28*(2), 95–110.
13. Kimani, N. J. (2019). Impact of large class sizes on competency-based curriculum implementation in Kenya. *African Journal of Education, 24*(4), 212–228.
14. Marzano, R. J. (2006). *Classroom assessment and grading that work*. Association for Supervision and Curriculum Development (ASCD).
15. Ministry of Education. (2017). *Basic Education Curriculum Framework*. Nairobi: Government Printer.
16. Mwangi, P., & Chege, M. (2020). Teacher preparedness in CBC implementation in Kenya. *Journal of Educational Research and Reviews, 10*(5), 125–138. https://doi.org/10.5897/JERR2020.3967

17. Mutiso, J. M. (2021). Evaluation of competency-based curriculum rollout in Kenya. *East African Education Studies, 12*(3), 143–157.
18. Muwagga, A. M., & Kakooza, J. B. (2021). The implementation challenges of competency-based curriculum in Uganda. *Makerere University Press.*
19. Niemi, H., & Isopahkala-Bouret, U. (2015). Teacher education in Finland: Innovations and future trends. *Journal of Teacher Education, 66*(3), 201–213. https://doi.org/10.3102/0034654314568497
20. Ngugi, G., & Wanjiru, L. (2020). The role of infrastructure in CBC implementation in Kenya. *Educational Leadership and Policy Studies, 36*(2), 94–108.
21. Njoroge, A. (2022). Resource demands and challenges in the CBC system. *Education Research Journal, 44*(1), 56–70.
22. National Institute of Statistics Rwanda. (2018). *Rwanda's education and workforce development report.* National Institute of Statistics Rwanda.
23. Nyamwembe, M. S., & Ombati, C. O. (2020). The economic implications of CBC on Kenyan households. *Kenya Economic Review, 31*(4), 210–223.
24. Odhiambo, G. (2021). Policy alignment and the CBC rollout in Kenya. *International Journal of Educational Policy, 16*(2), 77–89.
25. Odongo, M. S., & Okoth, D. (2020). Challenges facing teachers in CBC transition in Kenya. *Journal of Teacher Education and Training, 9*(3), 121–135.
26. OECD. (2012). *Equity and quality in education: Supporting disadvantaged students and schools.* OECD Publishing.
27. Otieno, M., & Cheruiyot, K. (2020). The digital divide and CBC implementation in Kenya. *Information and Communication Technology Journal, 15*(4), 233–245.
28. Otieno, P., & Njoroge, W. (2021). Overcrowded classrooms and the CBC framework in Kenya. *Journal of African Education, 19*(1), 65–77.
29. Owino, E. O., & Ndiku, M. (2021). Infrastructural challenges in the competency-based curriculum. *East African Journal of Education Research, 27*(2), 150–162.
30. Sahlberg, P. (2015). *Finnish lessons: What can the world learn from educational change in Finland?* Teachers College Press.
31. Schleicher, A. (2018). *World class: How to build a 21st-century school system.* OECD Publishing.
32. Sifuna, D. (2019). Educational reform and curriculum challenges in Kenya. *Nairobi University Press.*

33. Spady, W. G. (1994). *Outcomes-based education: Critical issues and answers.* American Association of School Administrators.
34. Spaull, N. (2019). Lessons from South Africa's CBC experience: Insights for Kenya. *Journal of Comparative Education, 18*(2), 129–142.
35. Trilling, B., & Fadel, C. (2009). *21st-century skills: Learning for life in our times.* Jossey-Bass.
36. Wanjiru, T., & Mugo, E. (2018). Facility gaps in Kenyan schools and CBC implementation. *Infrastructure in Education Journal, 7*(3), 110–123.
37. Wanjohi, J., & Muthoni, R. (2020). Teacher training and CBC implementation effectiveness in Kenya. *Kenya Teacher Journal, 21*(2), 143–156.
38. Waweru, N. (2019). Parental resistance to CBC costs in Kenya. *Social and Economic Studies, 29*(4), 65–78.

www.ingramcontent.com/pod-product-compliance
Lightning Source LLC
LaVergne TN
LVHW010459160826
845677LV00012B/2566

* 9 7 9 8 8 9 2 4 8 7 9 0 0 *